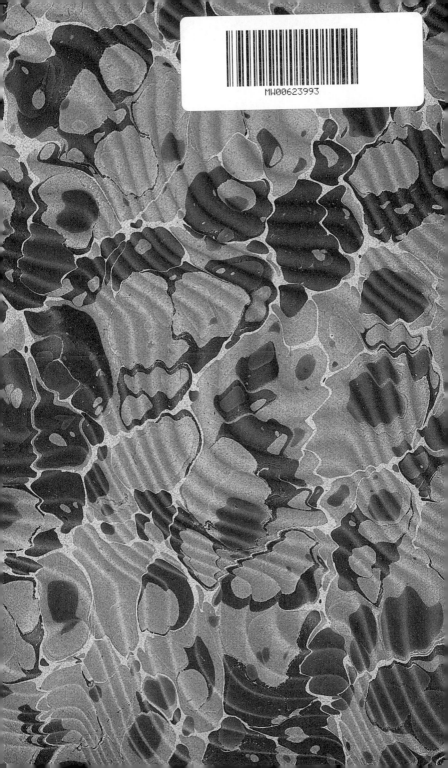

MW00623993

The Poetry of Home

THE POETRY OF HOME

Collected
by
Charlotte
Moss

VOLUME I

Boxwood Press · 1998

New York

First published in the United States of America
November, 1998
by
Boxwood Press
New York, NY

Compilation copyright © 1998 Charlotte Moss
Preface copyright © 1998 Margaret Kennedy
Introduction copyright © 1998 Suzanne Fox

FIRST EDITION

for my brother Ed

*W*hy? Why a book of quotations on rooms and houses? That's actually the easy question to answer. The difficult issue was when to stop, create a little book and move on.

Reading is one of my passions and as a part of making the time even more memorable, even at this age, I am still writing book reports. I record each book – a few thoughts, ideas or quotes to remember it by. Sometimes it's the story, more often than not it's the people, the places they inhabit or distant places traveled to. When Lesley Blanche wrote her cookbook, From Wilder Shores, The Tables of My Travels, she explained that by cooking a dish from a particular country she could get there spiritually and "recapture the rapture". The quotations here allow me to do just that.

It is my hope that by sharing the distilled essence of some of my reading you too will be inspired to pursue some of these volumes for the pure enjoyment of reading or to seek an expanded view of how you might shape your own home.

To my husband Barry, thank you for your infinite encouragement and patience. Thanks to all of the writers that have and those who will continue to create inspiring reading. And thank you Ricky. Ricky Spears has managed the publishing of this book as if it were his own.

Charlotte Moss

Table of Contents

Who among us has never been struck, upon entering a room for the first time, by its particular atmosphere, the undefinable perfume given off by it? Doesn't this effluvia of sensation seem to carry with it the memory of actions, silences, and emotions to which the room has been witness? Why wouldn't its walls have recorded and stored away all the emotional vibrations given off by its successive occupants and visitors? Both metaphor and psychic catalyst, a room always seems to reveal to us a specific psychological and spiritual universe.

Robert Polidori

Preface

Studying the lean, shimmering watercolors of Turner, I have learned that a few washes and terse brush strokes have the power to conjure up views of Venice more immediate and evocative than any photograph could. At the same time that he reduces landscape to its bare bones, this visionary artist heightens our perception of the scene. In similarly succinct fashion, a great writer can in two or three vivid sentences sketch the ambiance of a particular place and put us there.

Interior designer Charlotte Moss has been savoring just such painterly descriptions of homes for years. Her passion for reading, as well as her love of comely, inviting interiors inevitably compelled Charlotte to note favorite word images in her journals. She draws upon memorable passages as inspiration for her decorating.

Combining verbal and visual clues found in a biography of Mona Bismarck, Charlotte translated the stylish socialite's bedroom on Capri into a room for New York's Kips Bay Showhouse, featuring a fantastical bed capped by a tole umbrella. From snippets of text and memories of travel in France, Charlotte envisioned the interiors of the long-empty Hameau (Hamlet) at Versailles then produced an informed version of its dining room for a showhouse in Richmond, Virginia. When I invited Charlotte to create a vignette of Edith Wharton's study for an exhibition at the National Portrait Gallery in Washington, I discovered she not only owned every book ever written by or about the Gilded Age author, but she also shared Wharton's birthdate! Naturally, this well-read designer knew exactly what to do.

Charlotte Moss is a believer in the power of words to detonate memory and propel a reader into another place. The quotes in this collection were culled from her favorite observations of rooms both real and fictional. Perhaps they will nudge your imagination, connecting you to the fragrance, the feel, the poetry of home.

Margaret Kennedy, Editor, House Beautiful

Introduction

Homes can be made of brick and mortar, plaster and plank, fiber and glass. These actual homes are warmed by fires of real logs, popping and hissing with resin, and filled with real objects, from the luminous creamware plate discovered in a tiny old shop to the slightly awful cushion an aunt needlepointed as a wedding gift. They're scented with real roses, paid for with real dollars, and surrounded by real landscape, be it gorgeous or ugly, urban or bucolic. They're made even more insistently material by the inevitable intrusion of real dust, real clutter, real cracks, real breakages. Despite these flaws, there's absolutely no doubt that real rooms, made of real objects, are marvelous, even magical, things.

But magical rooms can also be made of words. At first words might seem to be lackluster tools for capturing the essence of home: the rich, russety colors of an old oriental rug, the satisfying *squoosh* as a down-filled cushion gives under your weight, the scent of rosemary drifting in from the kitchen garden, the sight of a child sleeping, the unseen yet comforting presence of a spouse somewhere in another room. Yet immaterial and evanescent as it may be, language can nevertheless evoke a sense of place so vivid that we feel, reading them, that we have walked over a threshold into an enchanting space, an interior more memorable and somehow more "real" than many we have visited in the flesh. These literary homes may not be able to shelter us from the elements, but they enjoy several undoubted advantages over the real thing. Their charm and comfort are limited only by the writer's imagination. Their curtains do not fade, nor their slipcovers go out of style; unlike actual homes, literary ones involve no maintenance, and whatever cracks they may have are emphatically not our problem. Visits to literary rooms require no impractical travel, just an armchair, a few spare hours, and perhaps a cup of Earl Grey. Best of all, they demand no invitation: we are as welcome to roam through the grandeur of Chatsworth as we are to visit Jane Eyre's humble rural cottage.

As its title implies, this small anthology celebrates the richness of rooms made out of words – quite literally, the poetry of home, the capacity of language to evoke the memory and dream, the texture and scent, the loss or anticipation, all of the intimate pleasures and passions of domestic life. The excerpts within *The Poetry of Home* muse, among other subjects, on the mysterious sense of passion people feel for a home, the influence of landscapes on the houses that inhabit them, the rewards and rigors of housekeeping, and the particular genius both women and the English seem to have for creating memorable interiors.

Emotional resonance is the pre-eminent quality

of the selections in *The Poetry of Home*, though variety runs it a close second. This small anthology is the literary equivalent of a grand old country house, full of nooks and crannies and rooms of every imaginable size, purpose, and style; each turn in a hallway, each open door, offers a new surprise, and the reader can wander at will sampling its treasures. Selections have been chosen from centuries of authors, from Cicero to a handful of contemporary writers, who together represent both high and low art, fiction and nonfiction. Some of the quotations here are succinct – E.B. White's ruefully terse observation that "Home was quite a place when people stayed there," for example – while others are lengthy (Poe's description of rooms in *The Masque of the Red Death* runs for several pages). Some excerpts attempt to capture universal truth about the nature of home, others to evoke only one particular place. Some are the result of hours of labor, as a great writer struggled first to imagine and then to describe the particular interior that perfectly represented a character's complex essential nature; others, jotted off in journals or letters, are utterly candid and unrehearsed. Together, these excerpts pay sometimes poignant, sometimes playful witness to the importance home has as both reality and symbol, and to the magic that results when the power of language is married to the richness and mystery of the idea of home.

Here, as just one example of this magic, is a scene from Edith Wharton's classic novel *The House of Mirth*. Wharton was both an accomplished decorator and a woman exquisitely aware of the subtle nuances of interiors. The homes she invented in *The House of Mirth* fascinate not only because their creator excels at using detail to capture the essential nature of a space – the confident relaxation of a bachelor's flat, the gilt-edged desperation of the hotel suite of a woman too fresh on the social scene to even be called *nouveau* – but also because they pierce right to the heart of a character's life. In this scene, which occurs near the start of the novel, Lily Bart visits Bellomont, the country estate of wealthy friends. Her hosts are plump, indolent, vulgar, and ultimately cruel. But they have more than enough money, and just enough sensibility, to elevate domestic life to a minor art form, and to create, for even their least important guest, a pervading sense of luxury and comfort.

> Everything in her surroundings ministered to a feeling of ease and amenity. The windows stood open to the sparkling freshness of the September morning, and between the yellow boughs she caught a perspective of hedges and parterres leading by degrees of lessening formality to the free undulations of the park. Her maid kindled a little fire on the hearth, and it contended cheerfully with the sunlight which slanted across the moss-green carpet and caressed the curved sides of an old marquetry desk. Near the bed stood a table holding her breakfast-tray, with its harmonious porcelain and silver, a handful of violets in a slender glass, and the morning paper folded beneath her letters.

Lily's means are as limited as her tastes are extravagant, and her stay at Bellomont is not a relaxed visit but a last-ditch battle in a long (and futile) campaign to win a wealthy husband. Still, the beauty of this room–the abundance of light and space, the impeccable but unobtrusive service, the appeal to virtually every sense, the illusion that the very world outside can be controlled for the guests' enjoyment–is potently seductive. It is the addictive pull of rooms like this, and all the beauty, ease, and refinement they so perfectly symbolize, that ultimately dooms Lily Bart. She can neither afford to live in such homes, nor bear to live in the homes she can afford. Readers may feel superior in the face of Lily's dubious values. But it is both a measure of Wharton's gift for evocation, and a testament to the power of the word to create a compelling interior, that we are just as enchanted as she is when we encounter that green and stately view, that crackling little fire, that handful of violets.

Like Lily Bart's guest room, many of the interiors described in *The Poetry of Home* are beautiful, both in their language and in the sights, scents, and textures they evoke. Yet this collection proves that literary rooms can be compelling even when they are poor and spare. Here, as evidence, are the words of a very different kind of heroine, Charlotte Brontë's unforgettable Jane Eyre. Jane is plain where Lily is gorgeous, blunt where Lily is subtle, unswervingly true to her own integrity where Lily, like a butterfly, first lights on and then flits away from wisdom. As governess, Jane Eyre visits luxurious residences that come with a crippling price tag. But unlike Lily Bart, she resists their dangerous comforts. Here, she has just moved into a tiny dwelling that is part of her compensation as teacher in a drab industrial town.

> My home, then – when I at last find a home – is a cottage: a little room with white-washed walls, and a sanded floor; containing four painted chairs and a table, a clock, a cupboard, with two or three plates and dishes, and a set of tea-things in delf. Above, a chamber of the same dimensions as the kitchen, with a deal bedstead, and chest of drawers; small, yet too large to be filled with my scanty wardrobe. . . .

No tray sits on Jane Eyre's bed; no maid waits, obligingly off-stage, to clean the table or sweep the bare floor. And yet underneath its modesty a kind of abundance does reside in this literary room – an abundance, you might say, of truth. Everything in Jane Eyre's home is exactly as it seems. She may have nothing, but she has nothing to lose; she's in debt to no false friend, up for auction to no boorish prospective husband. Charlotte Brontë had none of Wharton's training in the art of the interior, nor any of her opportunity to see glorious homes (for most of her sadly short life, Brontë lived in a dour parsonage-house amid the haunting but forbidding Yorkshire moors). Yet she, like Wharton, is a master at furnishing an imaginary room to express the complex heart of a fictional life.

As Brontë and Wharton (and Jane Austen, Honoré de Balzac, Virginia Woolf, Henry James, and scores of other writers) knew, and as this anthology proves, fictional rooms give us an intimate sense of characters' tastes, fears, and souls. Sometimes, as in J.M. Barrie's *Peter Pan*, they sparkle delightfully with effervescent–or in this case, you might correctly say incandescent–personality:

> There was one recess in the wall, no larger than a bird-cage, which was the private apartment of Tinker Bell. It could be shut off from the rest of the home by a tiny curtain, which Tink, who was most fastidious, always kept drawn when dressing or undressing. No woman, however large, could have had a more exquisite boudoir and bedchamber combined. The couch, as she always called it, was a genuine Queen Mab, with club legs; and she varied the bed-spreads according to what fruit-blossom was in season. Her mirror was a Puss-in-Boots, of which there are now only three, unchipped, known to the fairy dealers; the wash-stand was pie-crust and reversible, the chest of drawers an authentic Charming the Sixth, and the carpet and rugs of the best (the early) period of Margery and Robin. There was a chandelier from Tiddlywinks for the look of the thing, but of course she lit the residence herself. Tink was very contemptuous of the rest of the house, as indeed was perhaps inevitable, and her chamber, though beautiful, looked rather conceited, having the appearance of a nose permanently turned up.

Sometimes, instead – as in Edgar Allan Poe's *The Fall of the House of Usher* – they reflect a gloom so dense it seems to pervade every inch of available space, like a silent but noxious mist.

> Sleep came not near my couch – while the hours waned and waned away. I struggled to reason off the nervousness which had dominion over me. I endeavored to believe that much, if not all of what I felt, was due to the bewildering influence of the gloomy furniture of the room – of the dark and tattered draperies, which, tortured into motion by the breath of a rising tempest, swayed fitfully to and fro upon the walls, and rustled uneasily about the decorations of the bed.

Homes created with words tell us not only what a space looks like, but how a character inhabits it – a fact that is often as telling as the furnishings themselves. Lily Bart is an eternal visitor; Jane Eyre inhabits her small cottage, and later her marital home, with total security. Some characters – Frances Hodgson Burnett's Sarah Crewe, for example, or, below, newlywed Meg Brooke from Louisa May Alcott's *Little Women* – reside in inadequate dwellings contentedly.

> It was a tiny house, with a little garden behind, and a lawn about as big as a pocket-handkerchief in front.... But inside, it was altogether charming, and the happy bride saw no fault from garret to cellar. To be sure, the hall was so narrow, it was fortunate that they had no piano, for one never could have been got in whole; the dining-room was so small

that six people were a tight fit; and the kitchen stairs seemed built for the express purpose of precipitating both servants and china pell-mell into the coal-bin. But once get used to these slight blemishes, and nothing could be more complete, for good sense and good taste had presided over the furnishings, and the result was highly satisfactory. There were no marble-topped tables, long mirrors, or lace curtains in the little parlor, but simple furniture, plenty of books, a fine picture or two, a stand of flowers in the bay-window, and scattered all about, the pretty gifts which came from friendly hands, and were the fair-er for the loving messages they brought.

Others, like Jane Austen's great comic creation Mrs. Dashwood, fairly tremble with the need to make a sufficient space grand.

"As for the house itself, to be sure," said she, "it is too small for our family; but we will make ourselves tolerably comfortable for the pre-sent, as it is too late in the year for improve-ments. Perhaps in the spring, if I have plenty of money, as I dare say I shall, we may think about building. These parlours are both too small for such parties of our friends as I hope to see often collected here; and I have some thoughts of throwing the passage into one of them, with perhaps a part of the other, and so leave the remainder of that other for an entrance; this, with a new drawing-room, which may be easily added, and a bed-cham-ber and garret above, will make it a very snug little cottage. I could wish the stairs were handsome. But one must not expect every-thing; though I suppose it would be no diffi-cult matter to widen them. I shall see how much I am before-hand with the world in the spring, and we will plan our improvements accordingly."

In the meantime, till all these alterations could be made from the savings of an in-come of five hundred a year by a woman who had never saved in her life, they were wise enough to be contented with the house as it was; and each of them was busy in ar-ranging their particular concerns, and en-deavouring, by placing around them their books and other possessions, to form them-selves a home.

Not all literary rooms, of course, are fictional. Real people have written copiously about real rooms for centuries, expressing delight or dismay in their own or others' spaces. Sometimes (though not always) less imaginative than fictional interi-ors, the real spaces referred to in memoirs, jour-nals, letters, and biographies have the compensat-ing charm of giving us a fresh and distinctly per-sonal peek at home life as it is, and was, actually lived. Here, for example, is an excerpt from the centuries-old letter of a now-forgotten French-woman to a friend, describing her guest bedroom in a country home. Nothing could be further from Lily Bart's elegant chamber than the room as-signed to Madame Huguet de Graffigny:

It is the length and height of a large hall, with draughts coming in through a thousand slits around the windows, and which I will try to block if I live that long. This huge room has only one window, divided into three, as in the old days, with six shutters. The whitewashed paneling only partly remedies the sad effect of little light and no view. . . . The tapestry has large figures, but I don't know who they are and they are rather nasty. There is an alcove covered with very expensive-looking dress material, but unpleasant because ill-arranged. Old-fashioned armchairs, a chest of drawers, the only table is the bedside table, but in atonement I have a beautiful lacca povera dressing table. That is my bedroom, and I hate it. I have to say that . . . everything is disgustingly awful.

The house described is far from wonderful, and Madame de Graffigny is not famous. Yet this passage captures one of the many complex truths about the concept of home–the fact that it means different things to different people–and is, as well, quite delightful. Everyone has, at one time another, stayed in a place that felt miserably uncomfortable, but few have expressed their unease with quite the zesty gusto of Madame Huguet de Graffigny. Discovering that the home she is visiting is Voltaire's adds another layer of pleasure; there is something undeniably satisfying about finding that this towering intellect had domestic feet of clay.

The Poetry of Home is filled with such brief, vivid glimpses. Nancy Lancaster's biographer describes one of the socialite's country houses, which like all of Lancaster's dwellings was not only decorated with unequalled panache but also organized with a unique genius for hospitality (Madame Huguet de Graffigny would be green with envy):

> Everyone still awoke to a fire – the Kelmarsh housemaids slipped in and lit them at dawn – but radiators took the nip out of the air as well, and kept the rooms dry, while fitted carpets and rugs covered cold, bare floors. . . . At the foot of the generous four-poster beds there would be a chaise longue or a deep-seated chair with an ottoman to stretch out on before dinner. More chairs surrounded the fire. Each room had a desk with ample Kelmarsh Hall writing paper; each had books and a reading lamp at every possible resting spot. There was always a bottle of drinking water and a glass next to the bed, and every room always displayed an abundance of fresh flowers from the garden.

Osbert Sitwell evokes with hallucinatory vividness and deep longing the intense satisfaction of returning to the place that says "home":

> To me, home always meant Renishaw; and the summer took me there . . . I remember, every year, directly I arrived, running through the cool, pillared hall to the low, painted door a little taller than myself, opposite, and standing on tiptoe, so that the smell of the garden should come at me over it through the open window; the overwhelming and, as it seemed, living scent of stocks and clove carnations and tobacco-plant on a foundation of sun-warmed box hedges, the odor of any

component of which to this day carries me back to infancy, though never now do I obtain the full force it drew from that precise combination . . .

Lady Mount Temple, a nineteenth-century Englishwoman, affords us an amusing perspective on Victorian interior design, and demonstrates in the process her own delightfully staunch personality. Lady Mount Temple's rosy bower may sound dreadful to twentieth-century readers, but to continue to love one's frills and flourishes despite the undisguised contempt of fearsome Mr. Rossetti is character indeed:

> You remember our dear little house in Curzon Street; when we furnished it, nothing would please us but watered paper on the walls, garlands of roses tied with blue bows! Glazed chintzes with bunches of roses, so natural they looked, I thought, as if they had just been gathered (between you and me, I still think it was very pretty), and most lovely ornaments we had in perfect harmony, gilt pelicans or swans or candlesticks, Minton's imitation of Sevres, and gilt bows everywhere. One day Mr. Rossetti was dining alone with us, and instead of admiring my room and decorations, as I expected, he evidently could hardly sit at ease with them. I began then to ask him if it were possible to suggest improvements! "Well," he said frankly, "I should begin by burning everything you have got!"

Most of the excerpts collected in *The Poetry of Home* give similarly brief and isolated glimpses of their writers' days and residences, but sometimes, taken together, these accounts of home trace the arc and meaning of an entire life. One of the most moving examples is that of Vita Sackville-West, master gardener, writer, and friend of Virginia Woolf. Sackville-West's son, Nigel Nicolson, gives us a wonderful account of her discovery of Sissinghurst, on the grounds of which she and her husband Harold Nicolson later created one of England's most famous gardens:

> Sissinghurst appeared to my eyes (aged thirteen) quite impossible. It was the battered relic of an Elizabethan house in which not a single room was habitable. The future garden was a rubbish dump. The day was a wet one, and I trailed my mother between mountains of old tins and other unexplained humps from one brick fragment to another, each more derelict than the last. She suddenly turned to me, her mind made up: "I think we shall be very happy here." "But we haven't got to live here?" I said, appalled. "Yes, I think we can make something rather lovely out of it."

Later, we see the house take shape, guided by Vita's uncompromising sense of herself and her values, buffed by the gentle effects of the years:

> ... Vita, peering through a hole, at once exclaimed, "That will be my library, and this," waving a teaspoon around the walls, "will be my sitting room." Within a month or two it was, and it remained hers for the next thirty-two years. Few were ever admitted to it. ... She filled the room with her books and per-

sonal mementos – a stone from Persepolis, a photograph of Virginia, one of Pepita's dancing slippers – and as the wallpaper peeled and faded, and the velvet tassels slowly frayed, she would never allow them to be renewed. Her possessions must grow old with her. She must be surrounded by the evidence of time.

These are the only two excerpts in *The Poetry of Home* in which Vita Sackville-West is referred to directly, but she appears in several other selections as well, disguised as the character Orlando in Virginia Woolf's novel of the same name. The story behind this playful and wildly imaginative novel, which spans centuries of English history, is a touching one. Sackville-West had been born and raised in the huge mansion at Knole, in Kent; the great, rambling Elizabethan house was inextricably intertwined with her sense of her own identity, and the fact that as a woman she was barred from inheriting and owning it was a lifetime grief for her. With the writing of *Orlando*, Woolf returned this lost birthright to a beloved friend. Beginning as an Elizabethan male and ending as a twentieth-century British female, the character of Orlando, always recognizably Vita, plays at Knole, explores Knole, refurbishes Knole, entertains at Knole, and owns Knole, indisputably and triumphantly.

She fancied the rooms brightened as she came in; stirred, opened their eyes as if they had been dozing in her absence. She fancied, too, that hundreds and thousands of times as she had seen them, they never looked the same twice, as if so long a life as theirs had been stored in them a myriad moods which changed with winter and summer, bright weather and dark and her own fortunes and the people's characters who visited them. Polite, they always were to strangers, but a little weary; with her, they were entirely open and at their ease. Why not indeed?...They had nothing to conceal. She knew their sorrows and joys. She knew what age each part of them was and its little secrets – a hidden drawer, a concealed cupboard, of some deficiency perhaps, such as a part made up, or added later. They, too, knew her in all her moods and changes.

In *Orlando*, Woolf brings Sackville-West and her lost home together once more, in a union at once intimate and eternal.

Ah, but she knew where the heart of the house still beat. Gently opening a door, she stood on the threshold so that (as she fancied) the room could not see her and watched the tapestry rising and falling on the faint eternal breeze which never failed to move it...The heart still beat, she thought, however faint, however far withdrawn; the frail indomitable heart of the immense building.

The handwritten manuscript of *Orlando*, given as a gift by Virginia Woolf to Vita Sackville-West, lies today in a glass case in the hallway at Knole itself, where visitors can see it fittingly cradled in the house that inspired it. It is witness to the heart of a wonderful friendship and the mind of an extraor-

dinary genius; it is also, like so many of the selec-
tions in *The Poetry of Home*, a moving testament to
the power of words to create an imaginary home
just as magical, and as enduring, as the real thing.

Suzanne Fox

Hauntings

You do not say the same thing in one room as you say in another, that's how sensitive a room is.

Louis Kahn

When you buy an old house, you buy not only the bricks and mortar, tiles and chimneys, trees and lawns; you also buy ghosts. Of this I am firmly convinced. You buy an ectoplasmic mass of loves and hates and ardours and regrets, lingering on from the past.

Beverley Nichols

In houses which are old—the forms of whose very walls and pillars have taken body from the thoughts of men in a vanished time—we often sense something far more delicate, more unwordable, than the customary devices of a romanticist: the swish of a silken invisible dress on stairs once dustless, the fragrance of an unseen blossom of other years, the wraith momentarily given form in a begrimed mirror. These wordless perceptions can be due only, it seems, to something still retained in these walls; something crystallized from the energy of human emotion and the activities of human nerves. And, perhaps, it is because of this nameless life of memory and desire and, correlatively, because of a superior power of suggestion that, for those who are sensitive, the ruined houses have a fascination far exceeding that of the intact and inhabited structures. Within these damp vine-wrenched walls, these windows yawning from another position in time, these empty doors opening onto an age lost in space, there dwells still something unwordable, something for which the words "ghost" and "spirit" would be totally inadequate; something which is the ultimate reality from which these walls sprang, and which persists through the years; for though it came from the minds of men it has left a part of itself here.

Clarence John Laughlin

The worst of a modern stylish mansion is that it has no room for ghosts.

Oliver Wendell Holmes, Senior

In each instance the habitation reflected in a very special way the tone, the hidden music, as it were, of a woman, and a woman living alone, the sense of a deep loam of experience and taste expressed in the surroundings, the room a shell that reverberated with oceans and tides and waves of the owner's past, the essence of a human life as it had lived itself into certain colors, objects d'art, and especially into many books.

May Sarton

Inside these walls one feels as much legitimate fear as pleasure. An armed prowler would not dare to stay here at night. No more than us would he like the chaos of the interior....How to convince yourself that this dungeon-like darkness, a rosewood headrest and the remains of a commode are not positively evil?

Colette

The red-room was a spare chamber, very seldom slept in....yet it was one of the largest and stateliest chambers in the mansion. A bed supported on massive pillars of mahogany, hung with curtains of deep red damask, stood out like a tabernacle in the centre; the two large windows, with their blinds always drawn down, were half shrouded in festoons and falls of similar drapery; the carpet was red; the table at the foot of the bed was covered with a crimson cloth; the walls were a soft fawn colour, with a blush of pink in it; the wardrobe, the toilet-table, the chairs were of darkly polished old mahogany. Out of these deep surrounding shades rose high, and glared white, the piled-up mattresses and pillows of the bed, spread with a snowy Marseilles counterpane. Scarcely less prominent was an ample, cushioned easy-chair near the head of the bed, also white, with a footstool before it; and looking, I thought, like a pale throne.

This room was chill, because it seldom had a fire; it was silent, because remote from the nursery and kitchens; solemn, because it was known to be so seldom entered....Mr. Reed had been dead nine years: it was in this chamber that he breathed his last; here he lay in state; hence his coffin was borne by the undertaker's men; and, since that day, a sense of dreary consequence had guarded it from frequent intrusion.

Charlotte Brontë

I had been passing alone, on horseback, through a singularly dreary tract of country; and at length found myself, as the shades of evening drew on, within view of the melancholy House of Usher. I knew not how it was – but, with the first glimpse of the building, a sense of insufferable gloom pervaded my spirit. . . . I looked upon the scene before me – upon the mere house, and the simple landscape features of the domain – upon the bleak walls – upon the vacant eyelike windows – upon a few rank sedges – and upon a few white trunks of decayed trees – with an utter depression of soul which I can compare to no earthly sensation more properly than to the after-dream of a reveler upon opium. . . . What was it – I paused to think – what was it that so unnerved me in the contemplation of the House of Usher?

Edgar Allan Poe

One family only had lived within her walls. One family who had given her life. They had been born there, they had loved, they had quarreled, they had suffered, they had died. And out of these emotions she had woven a personality for herself, she had become what their thoughts and their desires had made her.

Daphne du Maurier

If you were to ask what is most important in a home, I would say memories.

Lillian Gish

Take an inventory of a house, leaving out the visuals. Count the closet's dull odor, the floor's wooden creak, the smug smell of cleanser around a sink. Every house has a Hansel-and-Gretel trail of these sensory bread crumbs that lead from the front door to the attic. It doesn't take a supernatural, fairy-tale awareness to pick.up on this dimension of a house: it's a perception built right into the subconscious. Those familiar smells and sounds, rather than the rooms' appearance, detonate the memory.

Jody Shields

Gauzy shadows moved on the ceiling. In the stillness, the dry sound of a chrysanthemum petal falling upon the marble of a table made one's nerves twang.

Vladimir Nabokov

She fancied the rooms brightened as she came in; stirred, opened their eyes as if they had been dozing in her absence. She fancied, too, that hundreds and thousands of times as she had seen them, they never looked the same twice, as if so long a life as theirs had been stored in them a myriad moods which changed with winter and summer, bright weather and dark and her own fortunes and the people's characters who visited them. Polite, they always were to strangers, but a little weary; with her, they were entirely open and at their ease. Why not indeed?...They had nothing to conceal. She knew their sorrows and joys. She knew what age each part of them was and its little secrets–a hidden drawer, a concealed cupboard, of some deficiency perhaps, such as a part made up, or added later. They, too, knew her in all her moods and changes.

Virginia Woolf

It was zero this morning. I have a fire burning in my study, yellow roses and mimosa on my desk. There is an atmosphere of festival, of release, in the house. We are one, the house and I, and I am happy to be alone–time to think, time to be.

May Sarton

Our house was not unsentient matter–it had a heart and a soul, and eyes to see with; and approvals and solicitudes and deep sympathies; it was of us, and we were in its confidence and lived in its grace and in the peace of its benedictions. We never came home from an absence that its face did not light up and speak out in eloquent welcome–and we could not enter it unmoved.

Samuel Clemens (Mark Twain)

All right, listen: late that afternoon when I woke up rain was at the window and on the roof; a kind of silence, if I may say, was walking through the house, and, like most silence, it was not silent at all: it rapped on the doors, echoed in the clocks, creaked on the stairs, leaned forward to peer into my face and explode.

Truman Capote

The furniture was lodging house. Not a single good piece...but darling, it was thrilling, Shaw was there. In the garden hut there he was still, in the shape of the ashes, on the rose bed and garden paths, white ashes....

Harold Nicolson, writing to his wife Virginia Sackville-West about a visit to George Bernard Shaw's longtime residence, Shaw's Corner

           .... Elated
Almost to the brink of fear – how can
the act of entering not alter, and ruin
in altering, what one loves for having been

until this instant wholly uninfected
by oneself? – you pause, and at the threshold
of possession, you observe the sacred

coal fire on the grate, the elbowed
stovepipe, the meal dish and the bed
of a household animal; the sideboard

in the adjoining room, a reredos
of snapshots, postcards, mementos
from all over, the unself-conscious

showpiece of a lifetime that must
have – otherwise why, as you paused
just now, that tremor of an unforced

happiness? – been happy.

Amy Clampitt, on the home of Samuel Taylor Coleridge

From the uncertainties of this world, this age, we turn to the only certainties – the things upon which our senses seize, however briefly; the things that delight our eyes, our ears, our skin, and to the magic aura created about these things by memory–that so carefully and subtly magnifies the emotionally significant phases of experience, and suppresses all the rest....So it is that those who feel, and know, something of the mystery and magic of the old ruined houses of Louisiana find in them more than the satisfaction of mere antiquarian curiosity; find, instead, unique stimulants to vision, and to memory; and, as well, what might roughly be termed a metaphysical and poetic adventure.

Clarence John Laughlin

The house was large, topped by a lofty garret. The steep gradient of the street compelled the coach-houses, stables, and poultry-house, the laundry and dairy, to huddle on a lower level all round a closed courtyard. Both house and garden are living still, I know; but what of that, if the magic has deserted them? If the secret is lost that opened to me a whole world–light, scents, birds and trees in perfect harmony, the murmur of human voices now silent for ever–a world of which I have ceased to be worthy?

Colette

Sleep came not near my couch–while the hours waned and waned away. I struggled to reason off the nervousness which had dominion over me. I endeavored to believe that much, if not all of what I felt, was due to the bewildering influence of the gloomy furniture of the room–of the dark and tattered draperies, which, tortured into motion by the breath of a rising tempest, swayed fitfully to and fro upon the walls, and rustled uneasily about the decorations of the bed.

Edgar Allan Poe

Gwenda stood there staring a long time, then she went shakily over to the bed and sat down on it.

Here she was in a house that she had never been in before, in a country she had never visited –and only two days ago she had lain in bed imagining a paper for this very room–and the paper she had imagined corresponded exactly with the paper that had once hung on the walls....

She could explain the garden path and the connecting door as coincidence–but there couldn't be a coincidence about this–you couldn't conceivably imagine a wallpaper of such a distinctive design and then find one exactly as you had imagined it....No, there was some explanation that eluded her and that–yes, frightened her. Every now and then she was seeing, not forward, but back–back to some former state of the house. Any moment she might see something more–something she didn't want to see....The house frightened her...But was it is the house or herself?

Agatha Christie

In any new room, you want to let the house talk to you before you begin imposing your ideas on it. After all, what living space doesn't come with its own history and set of standards, whether the construction be old or new. You must listen to the walls, talk to the cupboards, hear what the floor-boards say.

Charlotte Moss

Houses are totally anthropomorphic for me. They're so themselves.

Frances Mayes

Ah, but she knew where the heart of the house still beat. Gently opening a door, she stood on the threshold so that (as she fancied) the room could not see her and watched the tapestry rising and falling on the faint eternal breeze which never failed to move it . . . The heart still beat, she thought, however faint, however far withdrawn; the frail in-domitable heart of the immense building.

Virginia Woolf

The first sight of the grand entrance hall suggests a much larger house. White arum lilies on the sweeping staircase are banked up, up, up towards the exuberantly painted ceiling, a great vault of puffy clouds and flying geese framed by an Ital-ianate balustrade. Curly wrought-iron banisters circle the landing. Over the stairwell hangs a pen-nant, a dull red and gold remembrance of kingly things past.

What makes this somber, spacious hall seem so exotic? Is it the towering sunflowers on the gilded spread-eagle tables? Or the chinoiserie screen, its miniature imperial figures echoing the red and gray-green servant's livery that the Duke himself has designed? Or the limpid light from the glassed in candles?

Suzy Menkes
writing on The Duke and Duchess of Windsor's Paris home

A Passion for A Place

We struck off through the trees and came out upon the open hillside. In the distance below us stretched the sea. Behind us lay the woods and the valley through which we had come. But nowhere was there a sign of any house. Nowhere at all. "Perhaps," I thought to myself, "it is a house of secrets, and has no wish to be disturbed." But I knew I should not rest until I had found it.

Daphne du Maurier on Menabilly,
the house which inspired the novel Rebecca

I want this place to look like a garden, but a garden in hell. I want everything that can be to be covered in lovely cotton material. Cotton! Cotton! Cotton!

Diana Vreeland,
commenting to Billy Baldwin on her Park Avenue apartment

Sissinghurst appeared to my eyes (aged thirteen) quite impossible. It was the battered relic of an Elizabethan house in which not a single room was habitable. The future garden was a rubbish dump. The day was a wet one, and I trailed my mother between mountains of old tins and other unexplained humps from one brick fragment to another, each more derelict than the last. She suddenly turned to me, her mind made up: "I think we shall be very happy here." "But we haven't got to live here?" I said, appalled. "Yes, I think we can make something rather lovely out of it."

Nigel Nicolson

They saw Argyll House "one particular March morning – one of those exquisite spring days when London takes on deep blue shadows and high skies, is quite Italian in fact. The almonds were out here and there as we walked – no, rushed – down to Chelsea, and there it stood! One look was enough and we were utterly determined to own it." Here, near the river and surrounded by its own gardens, was that rare thing, a country house in London. On this spring morning "its dark front [stood] in blue shadow. . . . the great door a striking contrast of grey white." Everything about its architecture seemed individual and graceful.

Kirsty McLeod on and with Sibyl Colefax

Friends sometimes think excessive the pleasure I get from my house in North Wales. . . . I love it above all inanimate objects, and above a good many animate ones, too. I love it incessantly. When I am at home I wander around its rooms gloatingly; when I am away I lie in my hotel dreaming of it. If people show me pictures of their children, I show them pictures of my house, and there is nothing on earth I would swap it for, except perhaps something by Giorgione.

Jan Morris

Sometimes a man hits upon a place to which he mysteriously feels that he belongs. Here is the home he has sought, and he will settle amid scenes that he has never seen before, among men he has never known, as though they were familiar to him from his birth. Here at last he finds rest.

W. Somerset Maugham

Some people grow to love their homes: my reaction was instantaneous. It was love at first sight, and from the moment that I stood under the archway, I knew that this place was destined to be mine. This place must belong to me.

Cecil Beaton writing on Ashcombe

That people could come into the world in a place they could not at first even name and had never known before; and that out of a nameless and unknown place they could grow and move around in it until its name they knew and called out with love, and call it HOME, and put the roots there and love others there; so that whenever they left this place they would sing homesick songs about it and write poems of yearning for it, like a lover. . . .

William Goyden

It is everything I long for.

Audrey Hepburn,
on her Swiss villa La Paisible ("the peaceful place")

You can't imagine how wonderful it feels to be in that house and in those greenhouses. You know that she loves every chair, you know that she feels tenderly about every single blossom, and you know that she rips out anything that she doesn't like, not with violence or cruelty but with the simple determination to eliminate it. Hers is a regime of no tolerance for the mediocre.

Billy Baldwin writing on Mrs. Paul Mellon's home in Virginia

The house had captivated him from the very first. In one of those gleaming motor cars, his passion for which so bemused his fellow author Henry James, he recalls saying, in Something of Myself, "That's her! The only she! Make an honest woman of her – quick!" We entered and felt her spirit – her Feng Shui – to be good. We went through every room and found no shadows of ancient regrets, stifled miseries, nor any menace.

On Rudyard Kipling's home, Bateman's

Home! That was what they meant, those caressing appeals, those soft touches wafted through the air, those invisible little hands pulling and tugging, all one way! Why, it must be quite close by him at that moment, his old home that he had hurriedly forsaken and never sought again, that day when he first found the river! And now it was sending out its scouts and its messengers to capture him and bring him in. Since his escape on that bright morning he had hardly given it a thought, so absorbed had he been in his new life, in all its pleasures, its surprises, its fresh and captivating experiences. Now, with a rush of old memories, how clearly it stood up before him, in the darkness!

Shabby indeed, and small and poorly furnished, and yet his, the home he had made for himself, the home he had been so happy to get back to after his day's work. And the home had been happy with him, too, evidently, and was missing him, and wanted him back, and was telling him so, through his nose, sorrowfully, reproachfully, but with no bitterness or anger; only with plaintive reminder that it was there, and wanted him.

Kenneth Grahame

I love the house not just as a thing, but as a concentration of emotions and sensations, contained within a receptacle which in its style, its stance, its materials, its degree of grandeur and its position on the map exactly represents all that I have most cherished or coveted in life.

Jan Morris

What a pretty place it was – or rather, how pretty I thought it! I suppose I should have thought any place so where I had spent eighteen happy years. But it was really pretty. A large, heavy, white house, in the simplest style, surrounded by fine oaks and elms, and tall massy shrubs. . . . This is the exact description of the home which, three years ago, it nearly broke my heart to leave. What a tearing up by the roots it was! I have pitied cabbage-plants and celery, and all transplantable things, ever since; though, in common with them, and with other vegetables, the first agony of the transportation being over, I have taken such firm and tenacious hold of my new soil, that I would not for the world be pulled up again, even to be restored to the old beloved ground.

Mary Russell Mitford

Growing up, I absorbed the Southern obsession with place, and place can seem to me somehow an extension of the self.

Frances Mayes

In my early life Mirador was the healing thing for me, the balm; it healed all of my early ills. It always had that effect on me. Haseley was the same for me later in life. Haseley too had the power to heal whatever ailed me.

Nancy Lancaster

It was late autumn twilight when we found it–on foot along a line of Scotch firs with views of forest on old woodland reaching up to a great sky. . . . suddenly the end of a brick building–a Tudor window –and nearby a golden stone tower. We crept nearer–a low range of buildings faced the tower and more at right angles–an ugly Victorian porch, ivy covered. But the place was full of magic and our fate was sealed. We must live and look at that tower. That was our first view of Old Buckhurst. The light had nearly faded. Our feet [were] drenched with dew. Fearful of being caught–we knew nothing of the owners–we peered at the old brick walls. How to find out about it all?

Sibyl Colefax

. . . . it was hard to shake off the haunting impression the house had made upon me. If only someone could live there and bring it back to life, someone with children, the sound of laughter and happiness once more. And why did a past that I had never known possess me so completely? Always the past, just out of reach, waiting to be recaptured.

Daphne du Maurier

After a time of trouble I found a likable flat which was to be my home. I had had a long need of one, so it was also my dear shelter. My daughter and I moved in one evening with two suitcases, two beds, three pots of bulbs, a kettle and tea things. We lit a brilliant fire in the seemly little grate with the dry slats the builder had left after making a big opening between the two public rooms. I lay in the firelight peacefully listening to pigeons on the roof . . . I listened, looked out on the trees beyond both windows and I was free and happy. . . . It was already so precious to me that its surface was almost my skin.

Florida Scott-Maxwell

I don't think very much about my house. I just enjoy it.

Fred Astaire

I remember, too, the pleasure with which I always arrived at the house, experiencing a curious attachment to the soil, a sympathy with the form of the country, with its trees and flowers, the frail blue spires of bluebells in May, or the harebells and toad-flax of August, which has never left me and has made me wonder at times whether my ancestors, in the building up of an estate through so many hundreds of years, and by the hunger and passion for this land which must have inspired them—for it was an estate gradually accumulated, not obtained by huge grants or the purchase of church property—had not bequeathed to me something still very real and active in my nature; this love seemed to me so much older than myself and so much part of me.

Osbert Sitwell

It stood in a great garden outside the city wall and was built on three sides around a large central court. The atrium was decorated in typically Arabic fashion with heavy carvings, rare Persian rugs and porcelain. The shape of this room had been suggested by the priceless gift of a lamp which had originally hung in the Great Mosque at Mecca. Her massive, carved bed was overhung with gauze-like drapes falling from a large coronet and all the rooms led on to the flat roof where the household sat on summer nights.

In the courtyard was a large oblong pool fed by water from the river. Four fountains bubbled gently to provide the soft sounds of trickling water. Doves fluttered from a dovecote, and Jane has planted trees—citrus, flowering hibiscus, pomegranate, mulberry and, to remind her of England, a pear tree, unheard of in Damascus. Climbing roses and jasmine scrambled in profusion up arches, along walls and over the little *kiosque* she had built, where she could sit and read.

Mary S. Lovell describing Jane Digby el Mezrab's Demascus home

Probably when another woman would be dreaming of love affairs, I dream of the delightful houses I have lived in.

Jane S. Smith quoting Elsie de Wolfe

Seasons and Years

Like the face of a clock, a home has its cycles, and reflects the passage of time even when much of what is in and around it seems unchanged. Sometimes striking and sometimes subtle, sometimes permanent and sometimes temporary, sometimes joyous and sometimes deeply poignant, the transformations of time give the house much of its mystery. Some rooms resist time and some rooms reflect it—but in either case, minutes, hours, days, months, seasons, and years work a mysterious magic in the home.

The initial mystery that attends any journey is: how did the traveler reach his starting point in the first place? How did I reach the window, the walls, the fireplace, the room itself; how do I happen to be beneath this ceiling and above this floor? Oh, that is a matter for conjecture, for argument pro and con, for research, supposition, dialectic!

Louise Bogan

Standing in the weeds around the auctioneer's truck: a bird's-eye maple bedroom set, a vanity with an oval mirror, a bed with a scrolled headboard, a dainty desk and straight-backed chair. Some dry rot. Sold: one hundred dollars.

Three houses on a farm tucked into the folds of the Grand River breaks: a stone house, a log cabin, a two-story frame with gabled roof. Each built with care, each placed farther above the flood stage, each built bigger to accommodate a growing family. Abandoned now, a patchwork quilt still on the attic bed, a well-worn whetsone by the kitchen door.

Kathleen Norris

... Vita, peering through a hole, at once exclaimed, "That will be my library, and this," waving a teaspoon around the walls, "will be my sitting room." Within a month or two it was, and it remained hers for the next thirty-two years. Few were ever admitted to it. ... She filled the room with her books and personal mementos—a stone from Persepolis, a photograph of Virginia, one of Pepita's dancing slippers—and as the wallpaper peeled and faded, and the velvet tassels slowly frayed, she would never allow them to be renewed. Her possessions must grow old with her. She must be surrounded by the evidence of time.

Nigel Nicolson

The house was left; the house was deserted. It was left like a shell on a sandhill to fill with dry salt grains now that life had left it. The long night seemed to have set in; the trifling airs, nibbling, the clammy breaths, fumbling, seemed to have triumphed. The saucepan had rusted and the mat decayed. Toads had nosed their way in. Idly, aimlessly, the swaying shawl hung to and fro. A thistle thrust itself between the tiles in the larder. The swallows nested in the drawing-room; the floor was strewn with straw; the plaster fell in shovelfuls; rafters were laid bare; rats carried off this and that to gnaw behind the wainscots....What power now could prevent the fertility, the insensibility, of nature?

Virginia Woolf

Dick's study upstairs...was full of his boyhood. She could trace the history of his past in its quaint relics and survivals, in the school-books lingering on his crowded shelves, the school-photographs and college-trophies hung among his latest treasures. All his success and failures, his exaltations and inconsistencies, were recorded in the warm huddled heterogeneous room.

Edith Wharton

When I wake early – and the birds wake me – I lie and watch the brass handles on the cupboard grow clear; then the basin; then the towel-horse. As each thing in the bedroom grows clear, my heart beats quicker. I feel my body harden...I feel its slopes, its thinness. I love to hear the gong roar through the house and the stir begin – here a thud, there a patter. Doors slam; water rushes.

Virginia Woolf

Now breakfast-rooms are all right in the morning when the sun streams in on the toast and mar-

malade, but by afternoon they seem to vanish a lit-
tle and to fill with a strange silvery light, their own
twilight; there is a kind of sadness in them then. . . .

Mary Norton

> First daylight on the bittersweet-hung
> sleeping porch at high summer : dew
> all over the lawn, sowing diamond-
> point-highlighted shadows:
> the hired man's shadow revolving
> along the walk, a flash of milkpails
> passing : no threat in sight. . . .

Amy Clampitt

Here is the house. It was the most lovely house I
have ever seen. Surrounded by noble and decayed
trees, gaunt in the evening dusk, there it stood –
aristocratic and desolate – memories of Scarlett
and Tara-ruins. The gallery was falling in – one wing
of the roof slumped awkwardly – the door swung
on broken hinges. I have never seen anything like
it. Some of the windows had no glass. Old bits of
material were stuck in the empty frames. From the
front hall we went into a sitting room. I don't know
why I say "sitting room," there was nowhere to sit.

Fulco di Verdura

Seventeen windows, each with heavy outside
shutters and elaborate inside windows with
swinging wooden panels, and seven doors to lock.
When I pulled in the shutters, each room was sud-
denly dark, except for combs of sunlight cast on

the floor. The doors have iron bars to hook in place, all except the portone, the big front door, which closes with the iron key and, I suppose, makes the elaborate locking of the other doors and windows moot, since a determined thief could easily batter his way in, despite the solid thumft, thumft of the lock turning twice. But the house has stood here empty through thirty winters; what's one more? Any thief who pushed into the dark house would find a lone bed, some linens, stove, fridge, and pots and pans.

Frances Mayes

It was early still, and the house was sleeping. But later, when the sun was high, there would come no wreath of smoke from the chimneys. The shutters would not be thrown back, nor the doors unfastened. No voices would sound within those darkened rooms. Menabilly would sleep on, like the sleeping beauty of the fairy tale, until someone would come to wake her.

Daphne du Maurier

It is time for a change. My spirits are lifted by the very idea of it – living by the sea, the rhythm of the tides, the long-held dream come true. For when I was looking for a house and finally came to Nelson, I looked first at the sea. I shall have two years before the move can be made – time to feel and think my way into it.

May Sarton

When we left the dining-room, she proposed to show me over the rest of the house; and I followed her upstairs and downstairs, admiring as I went, for all was well-arranged and handsome. The large front chambers I thought especially grand; and some of the third story rooms, though dark and low, were interesting from their air of antiquity. The furniture once appropriated to the lower apartments had from time to time been removed here, as fashions changed: and the imperfect light entering by their narrow casements showed bedsteads of a hundred years old; chests in oak or walnut, looking, with their strange carvings of palm branches and cherubs' heads, like types of the Hebrew ark; rows of venerable chairs, high-backed and narrow; stools still more antiquated, on whose cushioned tops were yet apparent traces of half-effaced embroideries, wrought by fingers that for two generations had been coffin-dust. All these relics gave to the third story of Thornfield Hall the aspect of a home of the past: a shrine to memory. I liked the hush, the gloom, the quaintness of these retreats in the day; but I by no means coveted a night's repose on one of those wide and heavy beds. . . .

Charlotte Brontë

An abbey! Yes, it was delightful to be really in an abbey! But she doubted, as she looked around the room, whether anything within her observation would have given her the consciousness. The furniture was in all the profusion and elegance of modern taste. The fireplace, where she had expected the ample width and ponderous carving of former times, was contracted to a Rumford, with slabs of plain though handsome marble, and ornaments over it of the prettiest English china. The windows, to which she looked with peculiar dependence, from having heard the general talk of his preserving them in their Gothic form with reverential care, were yet less what her fancy had portrayed. To be sure, the pointed arch was preserved –the form of them was Gothic–they might be even casements; but every pane was so large, so clear, so light! To an imagination which had hoped for the smallest divisions and the heaviest stone work, for painted glass, dirt, and cobwebs, the difference was very distressing.

Jane Austen

Houses of the best taste are like clothes of the best tailors–it takes their age to show us how good they are.

Henry James

There was Manderly, our Manderly, secretive and silent as it had always been, the grey stone shining in the moonlight of my dream, the mullioned windows reflecting the green lawns and the terrace. Time could not wreck the perfect symmetry of those walls, nor the site itself, a jewel in the hollow of a hand.

Moonlight can play odd tricks upon the fancy, even upon a dreamer's fancy. As I stood there, hushed and still, I could swear that the house was not an empty shell but lived and breathed as it had lived before.

Light came from the windows, the curtains blew softly in the night air, and there, in the library, the door would stand half open as we had left it, with my handkerchief on the table beside the bow of autumn roses.

Daphne du Maurier

She protected herself from the heat as if from an intruder. The parlor shutters were closed; the inner blinds, behind the long loose curtains, which descended from the tops of the windows to the floor (where they lay in brushed-aside folds) were pulled down tightly to the sills. All over the house, the blinds were down. The wallpaper in the parlor scrolled its elaborate varicolor pattern (its reds and golds and greens) over the walls, in an artificial dusk. The cottage piano became a shape more than an object; the bases and the cabinet photographs on the mantelpiece almost disappeared in the gloom; the carpet (never taken up, even in summer) lost its big islands of garlanded roses; the satin cushions on the wicker settee and the white doilies on the little tables alone showed up in the semi-darkness.

Louise Bogan

I looked with timorous joy toward a stately house: I saw a blackened ruin.

No need to cower behind a gate-post, indeed! – to peep up at chamber lattices, fearing life was astir behind them! No need to listen for doors opening–to fancy steps on the pavement or the gravel-walk! The lawn, the grounds were trodden and waste: the portal yawned void. The front was, as I had once seen it in a dream, but a shell-like wall, very high and very fragile looking, perforated with paneless windows: no roof, no battlements, no chimneys–all had crashed in.

And there was the solitude of death around it: the solitude of a lonesome wild.... In wandering around the shattered walls and through the devastated interior, I gathered evidence that the calamity was not of late occurrence. Winter snows, I thought, had drifted through that void arch; winter rains beaten in at those hollow casements; for, amidst the drenched piles of rubbish, spring had cherished vegetation: grass and weed grew here and there between the stones and fallen rafters.

Charlotte Brontë

The whole house stood, in winter, turned as cold as a tomb. The upper rooms smelled of cold plaster and cold wood. The parlor was shut; the piano stood shut and freezing against the wall; the lace curtains fell in starched frigid folds down to the cold grain of the carpet. The little padded books on the table, the lace doilies under them, the painted china vases, and the big pictures hanging against the big pattern of the wallpaper all looked distant, desolate, and to no purpose when the door was opened into the room's icy air.

Louise Bogan

There was a room there, set apart from the hallway by a red velvet rope. It was luxurious, subtle, glowing, still. Even to my unsophisticated eyes it was obviously a room from the past, but it hinted at human presence, as if its occupants had just by chance wandered casually away. The chair near the desk had been left slightly askew and a book lay open on its seat. What seemed to be the weakly golden sun of a misty afternoon slanted through the tall windows. The round, white-draped table was fully set. There was a book on the small desk, a clock on the mantel, even a dusty wine bottle stuck in a wooden stand.

Suzanne Fox

The library was almost the only surviving portion of the old manor-house at Bellomont; a long spacious room, revealing the traditions of the mother-country in its classically cased doors, the Dutch tiles of the chimney, and the elaborate hob-grate with its shining brass urns. A few family portraits of lantern-jawed gentlemen in tie-wigs and ladies with large head-dresses and small bodies hung between the shelves lined with pleasantly shabby books: books mostly contemporaneous with the ancestors in question and to which the subsequent Trenors had made no perceptible additions. The library at Bellomont was in fact never used for reading, though it had a certain popularity as a smoking-room or a quiet retreat for flirtation.

Edith Wharton

My most kind friend, Mr. Ruskin, will understand why I connect his name with the latest event that has befallen me: the leaving of the cottage that for thirty years had been my shelter. In truth, it was leaving me. All above the foundation seemed mouldering, like an old cheese, with damp and rottenness. The rain came dripping through the roof and streaming through the walls. The hailstones pattered upon my bed, through the casements, and the small panes rattled and fell to pieces every high wind...The poor cottage was crumbling around us, and if we had staid much longer we would have been buried in the ruins.

Mary Russell Mitford

How many times had I imagined this house – the family warmth and domestic order it represented! Fascinated, I assessed the decor, absorbing each table, chair, and object: a rack with straw hats, a pair of green gardening gloves next to a basket piled with sunglasses, a clutch of bright umbrellas in a brass stand. The rooms were attractively, if conventionally furnished: a few obligatory antique pieces relieved the eye of the monotony of the serviceable sofas, with their tightly woven wicker frames and smooth white cushions. Everything looked as if it had been eternally set in place – a comfortable, if unsensual room with an absence of fluidity.

Francesca Stanfill

Cold nights on the farm, a sock-shod
stove-warmed flatiron slid under
the covers, mornings a damascene-
sealed bizarrerie of fernwork
  decades ago now. . . .

damp sheets in Dorset, fog-hung
habitat of bronchitis, of long
hot soaks in the bathtub, of nothing
quite drying out till next summer:
  delicious to think of . . .

Amy Clampitt

Furnishings

At length, however, there was no room in the galleries for another table; no room on the tables for another cabinet; no room in the cabinet for another rose-bowl; no room in the bowl for another handful of potpourri; there was no room for anything anywhere; in short the house was furnished.

Virginia Woolf

"To express the things of the spirit in visible form": it's my belief that our spirits are most honestly expressed not by sofas, curtains, and carpets, but by the stack of favorite mysteries and gardening books on a side table, flowers on the windowsill, or porcelains displayed in the dining room. These "telling details" – our objects, bibelots, whatnots, and knickknacks – say the most about who we are. They are as honest as a diary.

Charlotte Moss

"You see," she said, "there could be a thick, soft blue Indian rug on the floor; and in that corner there could be a soft little sofa, with cushions to curl up on; and just over it could be a shelf full of books so that one could reach them easily; and there could be a fur rug before the fire, and hangings on the wall to cover up the whitewash, and pictures. They would have to be little ones, but they could be beautiful; and there could be a lamp with a deep rose-colored shade; and a table in the middle, with things to have tea with; and a fat little copper kettle singing on the hob; and the bed would be quite different. It could be made soft and covered with a lovely silk coverlet. It could be beautiful...."

"Oh, Sara!" cried Lottie; "I should like to live here!"

Frances Hodgkin Burnett

I then filled the hall with the three things that were essential to me in any room: real candlelight, wood fires, and lovely flowers.

Nancy Lancaster

With supernal grace, the rhythm of the staircase ascends – a very poem in wood.

Clarence John Laughlin

On each side of the shiny painted steps was a large blue china flower-pot on a bright yellow china stand. A spiky green plant filled each pot, and below the verandah ran a wide border of blue hydrangeas edged with more red geraniums.... the French windows of the drawing-rooms...gave glimpses, between swaying lace curtains, of glassy parquet floors islanded with chintz poufs, dwarf armchairs, and velvet tables covered with trifles in silver.

Edith Wharton

It was a charming room, oddly shaped to conform with the curve of the dome. The walls were papered in a pattern of ribbons and roses. There was a rocking horse in the corner and an oleograph of the Sacred Heart over the mantelpiece; the empty grate was hidden by a bunch of pampas grass and bulrushes; laid out on the top of the chest of drawers and carefully dusted were the collection of small presents which had been brought home to her at various times by her children, carved shell and lava, stamped leather, painted wood, china, bog oak, damascened silver, blue-john, alabaster, coral, the souvenirs of many holidays.

Evelyn Waugh

The apartments were so irregularly disposed that the vision embraced little more than one at a time. There was a sharp turn at every twenty or thirty yards, and at each turn a novel effect. To the right and left, in the middle of each wall, a tall and narrow Gothic window looked out upon a closed corridor which pursued the windings of the suite. These windows were of stained glass, whose colour varied in accordance with the prevailing hue of the decorations of the chamber into which it opened. That at the eastern extremity was hung, for example, in blue – and vividly blue were its windows. The second chamber was purple in its ornaments and tapestries, and here the panes were purple. The third was green throughout, and so were the casements. The fourth was furnished and lighted with orange – the fifth with white – the sixth with violet. The seventh apartment was closely shrouded in black velvet tapestries that hung all over the ceiling and down the walls, falling in heavy folds upon a carpet of the same material and hue. But in this chamber only the colour of the windows failed to correspond with the decorations. The panes here were scarlet—a deep blood colour.

Edgar Allan Poe

His flat, decorated in dark greens and pale greys, was furnished in a bold style typical of him: heavy candlesticks, solid fire-irons, a huge lump of crystal on the low table, the very chaste *appliqués*, the two large bushes of azaleas, one white, one pink, in porphyry pots. It is a phenomenon that the son of an ordinary Spanish boatman, a poor boy with no opportunity to glimpse the grand world, should be born with such innate taste.

Cecil Beaton writing on Cristobal Balenciaga's Paris apartment

Colours, like perfumes, affect the mind in very peculiar ways.

Walter Shaw Sparrow

The Coach House had a lightness to it, though it was completely stuffed with Nancy's things. Every surface was covered, both horizontal and vertical. Walls were packed with pictures, engravings of formal gardens, silhouettes, all of different shapes and sizes. The mirror over the fire had photographs and postcards wedged all around its frame: a card of Gilbert Stuart's "Skater," photos of

Nancy's dogs, her sons and her grandchildren. The firewood in the basket was cut small to fit the cottage fireplace, and the bark was removed like the crusts of sandwiches. There was as much furniture in the sitting room that could fit without seeming claustrophobic.

Robert Becker on Nancy Lancaster

It was a rosy room, hung with one of the new English chintzes, which also covered the deep sofa, and the bed with its rose-lined pillow-covers.... Ah, how she and Susan had...sewn and hammered...in the making of that airy monument!

Edith Wharton

The yellow of the carpet does not match the yellow moiré of the walls. But we have all experienced that happy moment when disparate elements are suddenly unified. These are moments of revelation and perfection. Sometimes, I think, decorators are apt to overdo the quest for absolute perfection. The odd touch of what I call asymmetry, whether in color or arrangement, can give added vitality, individuality, and, frequently, unexpected elegance to a room.

Manuel Canovas

Why do I remember this house as the happiest in my life?...now I realize it was the house wherein I began to read, wholeheartedly and with pleasure. It was the first house where bookshelves (in a narrow space between the dining room and the parlor) appeared as a part of the building; they went up to the ceiling, and were piled with my brother's books, mixed with the books my mother had acquired in one way or another...

Louise Bogan

A dog in the home is a piece of moving furniture.

Philippe de Rothschild commenting to Cecil Beaton

First a bookcase with a great many books in it; next a table that will keep steady when you write or work at it: then several chairs that you can move, and a bench that you can sit or lie upon: next a cupboard with drawers: next, unless either the bookcase or the cupboard are very beautiful with painting or carving, you will want pictures or engravings, such as you can afford, not only stop gaps, but real works of art on the wall; or else the wall itself must be ornamented with some beautiful restful patterns: we shall also want a vase or two to put flowers in which latter you must have sometimes, especially if you live in a town. Then there will be a fireplace, of course, which in our climate is bound to be the chief object in the room.

William Morris,
on the necessities that ought to furnish a room

The tall lamps were all lit, and Mr. Van der Luyden's orchids had been conspicuously disposed in various receptacles of modern porcelain and knobby silver. Mrs. Newland Archer's drawing-room was generally thought a great success. A gilt bamboo jardiniere, in which the primulas and cinerarias were punctually renewed, blocked access to a bay window (where the old-fashioned would have preferred a bronze reduction of the Venus de Milo); the sofas and arm-chairs of pale brocade were cleverly grouped around little plush tables densely covered with silver toys, porcelain animals, and efflorescent photograph-frames; and tall rosy-shaded lamps shot up like tropical flowers among the palms.

Edith Wharton

At the mention of a clergyman's study, perhaps, your too active imagination conjures up a perfect snuggery, where the general air of comfort is rescued from a secular character by strong ecclesiastical suggestions in the shape of the furniture, the pattern of the carpet, and the prints on the wall; where, if a nap is taken, it is in an easy-chair with a Gothic back, and the very feet rest on a warm and velvety simulation of church windows; where the pure art of rigorous English Protestantism smiles above the mantle-piece in the portrait of an eminent bishop, or a refined Anglican taste is indicated by a German print from Overbeck....But I must beg you to dismiss all such scenic prettiness, suitable as they may be to a clergyman's character and complexion; for I have to confess that Mr. Tryan's study was a very ugly little room indeed, with an ugly slap-dash pattern on the walls, an ugly carpet on the floor, and an ugly view of cottage roofs and cabbage-gardens from the window.

George Eliot

My furniture, part of which I made myself. . . . consisted of a bed, a table, a desk, three chairs, a looking-glass three inches in diameter, a pair of tongs and andirons, a kettle, a skillet, and a frying-pan, a dipper, a washbowl, two knives and forks, three plates, one cup, one spoon, a jug for oil, a jug for molasses, and a japanned lamp. None is so poor that he need sit on a pumpkin. That is shiftlessness.

Henry David Thoreau

A chair is a very difficult object. A skyscraper is almost easier. That is why Chippendale is famous.

Mies van der Rohe

I love it—I love it, and who shall dare
To chide me for loving that old Arm-chair?

Eliza Cook

What Deering admired most were the chairs around the table. They were Venetian peasant chairs in red enamel and gilt, with high ladder backs and rush seats. He liked them because they were so flattering to women, framing them like portraits.

Kathryn Chapman Harwood

Whichever way you use pattern, the only great pitfall to avoid is timidity. Many women, in a burst of decorating energy, will put up patterned walls, patterned curtains, patterned furniture, then screech to a halt and install plain carpeting. You must have the courage to go to the limit with pattern, have a figured carpet or a stencilled floor, or at least the regular, monotone pattern of waxed quarry tiles. And for good measure, heap that flowery sofa with cushions – dozens of them – in lots of tiny prints.

Billy Baldwin

There were India shawls suspended, curtainwise, in the parlour door, and curious fabrics, corresponding to Gertrude's metaphysical vision of an opera-cloak, tumbled about in the sitting places. There were pink silk blinds in the windows, by which the room was strangely bedimmed.

Henry James

She pointed to a wide arch corresponding to the window, and hung like it with a Tyrian-died curtain, now looped up. Mounting to it by two broad steps and looking through, I thought I caught a glimpse of a fairy place, so bright to my novice-eyes appeared the view beyond. Yet it was merely a very pretty drawing-room, and within it lay a boudoir, both spread with white carpets, on which seemed laid brilliant garlands of flowers; both ceiled with snowy mouldings of white grapes and vine-leaves, beneath which glowed in rich contrast crimson couches and ottomans; while the ornaments on the pale Parian mantel-piece were of sparkling Bohemian glass, ruby red; and between the windows large mirrors repeated the general blending of snow and fire.

Charlotte Brontë

The little villa-house where Pauline and Philippe de Rothschild live today was built in 1890; with its tall gothic stone walls, it is like a child's illustration to Walter Scott. Inside it is crammed with Napoleon III decorations, bead pictures, bead cushions, gold drawing-room furniture upholstered in scarlet brocade, flowered rugs on red carpets and colored glass panes in the verandah porch. Huge trumpet-shaped vases, filled with blossoms stand on the floor and there are pots of calceolarias and ferns. Miniatures in jeweled frames are mounted on velvet and displayed on easels.

Cecil Beaton

To collect anything, no matter what, is a healthy human impulse of a man and boy, and the longer and harder the search, the greater the joy of acquisition.

Agnes Repplier

His room was filled with a strange jumble of objects –a harmonium in a gothic case, an elephant's-foot wastepaper basket, a dome of wax fruit, two disproportionately large Sevres vases, framed drawings by Daumier–made all the more incongruous by the austere college furniture and the large luncheon table. His chimney-piece was covered with cards of invitation from London hostesses.

Evelyn Waugh

Everything in her surroundings ministered to a feeling of ease and amenity. The windows stood open to the sparkling freshness of the September morning, and between the yellow boughs she caught a perspective of hedges and parterres leading by degrees of lessening formality to the free undulations of the park. Her maid kindled a little fire on the hearth, and it contended cheerfully with the sunlight which slanted across the moss-green carpet and caressed the curved sides of an old marquetry desk. Near the bed stood a table holding her breakfast-tray, with its harmonious porcelain and silver, a handful of violets in a slender glass, and the morning paper folded beneath her letters.

Edith Wharton

"You'll want to see your room," said Jane. "We haven't put you in the proper spare room—it seemed so very vast and cold—but in one of the smaller ones. Here we are." She flung open the door of what seemed to Prudence, who was used to a boxlike, centrally-heated flat, a very large, bare-looking room with a bed in one corner, a chest of drawers, a chair and an old-fashioned marble-topped washstand. There were a few books on a little table by the bed, but no reading lamp, Prudence noticed quickly, just a light hanging rather too high up in the middle of the room. The floor was covered with shabby linoleum on which two small rugs had been placed in strategic positions, one by the bed and the other before a little looking-glass which hung on one wall.

Darling Jane, thought Prudence, noticing a rather rough arrangement of winter flowers in a little jar on the bedside table, a solitary rose, a few Michaelmas daisies and a dahlia.

Barbara Pym

It is the length and height of a large hall, with draughts coming in through a thousand slits around the windows, and which I will try to block if I live that long. This huge room has only one window, divided into three, as in the old days, with six shutters. The whitewashed paneling only partly remedies the sad effect of little light and no view. . . . The tapestry has large figures, but I don't know who they are and they are rather nasty. There is an alcove covered with very expensive-looking dress material, but unpleasant because ill-arranged. Old-fashioned armchairs, a chest of drawers, the only table is the bedside table, but in atonement I have a beautiful lacca povera dressing table. That is my bedroom, and I hate it. I have to say that . . . everything is disgustingly awful.

Madame Huguet de Graffigny,
describing her guest bedroom in the home of Voltaire

Here, in a thicket of stunted oaks, her verandahs spread themselves above the island-dotted waters. A winding drive led up between iron stages and blue glass balls embedded in mounds of geraniums to a front door of highly-varnished walnut under a striped verandah-roof; and behind it ran a narrow hall with a black and yellow star-patterned parquet floor, upon which opened four small square rooms with heavy flock-papers under ceilings on which an Italian house-painter had lavished all the divinities of Olympus.

Edith Wharton

One rubber-plant can never make a home,
Not even when combined with brush and comb,
And spoon, and fork, and knife,
And gramophone, and wife –
No! Something more is needed for a home.

Author unknown

You remember our dear little house in Curzon Street; when we furnished it, nothing would please us but watered paper on the walls, garlands of roses tied with blue bows! Glazed chintzes with bunches of roses, so natural they looked, I thought, as if they had just been gathered (between you and me, I still think it was very pretty), and most lovely ornaments we had in perfect harmony, gilt pelicans or swans or candlesticks, Minton's imitation of Sevres, and gilt bows everywhere. One day Mr. Rossetti was dining alone with us, and instead of admiring my room and decorations, as I expected, he evidently could hardly sit at ease with them. I began then to ask him if it were possible to suggest improvements! "Well," he said frankly, "I should begin by burning everything you have got!"

Lady Mount Temple

The light in the drawing room gave the illusion of a spring day. It bounced off the green damask curtains, the Louis XVI chairs covered with flowering tapestries, the malachite tables, and was reflected in the mirrors and the crystal objects scattered around the room. There were treasures everywhere. Fayum mortuary portraits with glazed eyes smiled down from the leaf-green walls onto enigmatic Egyptian sculptures; silver and gold ash trays seemed to throw sparks at the massive Empire crystal and bronze candelabra hanging from the ceiling; while the Aubusson carpet, covering the floor, was a field of verdant hues.

Patrick O'Higgins describing Helena Rubinstein's Paris Apartment

Pure white walls provided a background for touches of shock colour. In the inviting, casually arranged living-room were curtains of a stiff and gleaming rubber substance. Chairs covered in yellow chintz, an enormous orange leather couch and two armchairs in emerald green rubber. In the dining-room, small black bridge-like tables with glasstops were set before almond-green divans. The bedroom was done in a blistered lavender blue fabric. A footstool was made form the hipbones of an Argentinian horse.

Palmer White writing on Schiaparelli

"I've got a perfectly blissful and more or less permanent flat." The furniture is qualité de musée – such wonderful pieces. Her individual taste was most evident in the arrangement of this luminous residence. One cannot imagine it without her, so serene emanation of the *entente cordiale*, French in its sophisticated simplicity yet English in a certain cosiness and feeling for privacy. From the large square grey salon, pink curtained on the crosslights, one could glimpse the white muslin on her bed and there, in that small bedroom in an armchair by the window, her books were written.

Harold Acton
writing on Nancy Mitford's Paris Apartment she called "Mr. Street"

A Woman's Room

The main figure in the Home Front is the woman. It is she who must make the stand, rally her family around her like a general, and plant her own feet firmly on the home ground. Everything depends on her wisdom, her enthusiasm, her vision of what home can produce, what home can be.

Harper's Bazaar, May 1942

He looked round the Regency elegance of Prudence's sitting-room with a half-nervous, half-scornful expression on his face.

"Just the sort of place you ought to live in," he said at last. "Very Vogue and all that. Not quite my cup of tea, I'm afraid."

Barbara Pym

This was a woman's room, graceful, fragile, the room of someone who has chosen every particle of furniture with great care, so that each chair, each vase, each small infinitesimal thing should be in harmony with one another, and with her own personality. It was as though she who had arranged this room had said, "This I will have, and this, and this," taking piece by piece from the treasures in Manderly each object that pleased her best, ignoring the second-rate, the mediocre, laying her hand with sure and certain instinct only upon the best.

Daphne du Maurier

She could go there after anything unpleasant below, and find immediate consolation in some pursuit, or with some train of thought at hand.–Her plants, her books–of which she had been a collector, from the first hour of her commanding a shilling–her writing desk, and her works of charity and ingenuity, were all within her reach; or if indisposed for employment, if nothing but musing would do, she could scarcely see an object in that room which had not an interesting remembrance connected with it.–Everything was a friend, or bore her thoughts to a friend.…The room was most dear to her, and she would not have changed its furniture for the handsomest in the house, though what had been originally plain had suffered all the ill-usage of children.

Jane Austen

If I refer to the house as "she," it is because it seems very feminine to me, an indomitable grande dame gazing out to sea from her stronghold on the shores of Biscayne Bay.

Kathryn Chapman Harwood

Men would never have come to need an attic.
Keen collectors of glass or Roman coins build
Special cabinets for them, dote on, index

Each new specimen: only women cling to
Items out of their past they have no use for,
Can't name now what they couldn't bear
    to part with.

W.H. Auden

A man may build and decorate a beautiful house,
but it remains for a woman to make a home of it
for him.

Elsie de Wolfe

The first sleeping porch that I ever knew led a dou-
ble life. During the day it was a casual outdoor
room, but at night it was a magical place – espe-
cially to me, a shy eleven-year-old girl spending a
few weeks in the summer with her three older
cousins in an old white house in Fall River, Massa-
chusetts. At night on the sleeping porch I was part
of the cast. Every evening three studio couches
would be unfolded and made into double beds
with puffy pillows and thin cotton blankets. The
stage was set, then the dialogue began.

Dee Hardie

I have sometimes thought that a woman's nature
is like a great house full of rooms: there is the hall,
through which everyone passes in going in and
out; the sitting room, where members of the fam-
ily come and go as they list; but beyond that, far
beyond, are other rooms, the handles of whose
doors are never turned; no one knows the way to
them, no one knows whither they lead; and in the

innermost room, the holy of holies, the soul sits alone and waits for a footstep that never comes.

Edith Wharton

This room was all her own; she had taken it for herself and changed it so that, entering, one seemed to be in another house. She had lowered the ceiling, and the elaborate cornice which, in one form or another, graced every room, was lost to view; the walls, once paneled in brocade, were stripped and washed blue and spotted with innumerable little water-colors of fond association; the air was sweet with the fresh scent of flowers and musty pot-pourri; her library in soft leather covers, well-read books of poetry and piety, filled a small rosewood bookcase; the chimney-piece was covered with small personal treasures—an ivory Madonna, a plaster St. Joseph, posthumous miniatures of her three soldier brothers.

Evelyn Waugh

Nancy's recipe of elegance cum comfort furnished the room: chintz, petit point, an old painted side chair, a reupholstered bergère, a black lacquer chest of drawers given her by Lady Beatty, a Dutch boeketten still life, a marquetry desk, a whole collection of gold-topped dressing table accessories and eighteenth-century gilded tortoise-shell boxes. Loelia Westminster thought Nancy's bedroom an "enchantment" and "as rural-seeming as anything this side of the Wiltshire border."

Robert Becker on Nancy Lancaster

When it rained or snowed, Charles would direct his horse over the shortcuts.... every night he would come home to a glowing fire, the table set, the furniture arranged comfortably and a charming woman, neatly dressed, smelling so fresh you wondered where the fragrance came from and whether it wasn't her skin lending the scent to her petticoat. She wanted two large vases of blue glass on her fireplace, and awhile later, an ivory work-box with a vermeil thimble. The less Charles understood those elegant touches, the more he responded to their attraction. They added something to his sensual pleasures and the sweetness of his home. It was as if gold dust were being spread all along the narrow path of his life.

Gustave Flaubert

She made home happy, those few words I read
Within a churchyard, written on a stone.

Henry Coyle

There was one recess in the wall, no larger than a bird-cage, which was the private apartment of Tinker Bell. It could be shut off from the rest of the home by a tiny curtain, which Tink, who was most fastidious, always kept drawn when dressing or undressing. No woman, however large, could have had a more exquisite boudoir and bedchamber combined. The couch, as she always called it, was a genuine Queen Mab, with club legs; and she varied the bed-spreads according to what fruit-blossom was in season. Her mirror was a Puss-in-Boots, of which there are now only three, unchipped, known to the fairy dealers; the wash-stand was pie-crust and reversible, the chest of drawers an authentic Charming the Sixth, and the carpet and rugs of the best (the early) period of Margery and Robin. There was a chandelier from Tiddlywinks for the look of the thing, but of course she lit the residence herself. Tink was very contemptuous of the rest of the house, as indeed was perhaps inevitable, and her chamber, though beautiful, looked rather conceited, having the appearance of a nose permanently turned up.

J.M. Barrie

He came into his mother's room. It was as the abode of a fairy to him – a mystic chamber of splendour and delights. There in the wardrobe hung those wonderful robes – pink and blue and many-tinted. There was the jewel case, silver-clasped, and the wondrous bronze hand on the dressing-table, glistening all over with a hundred rings.

William Makepeace Thackeray

"Now, my dear Dorothea, I wish you to favour me by pointing out which room you would like to have as your boudoir," said Mr. Casaubon....

The chairs and tables were thin-legged and easy to upset. It was a room where one might fancy the ghost of a tight-lipped lady revisiting the scene of her embroidery. A light bookcase contained duodecimo volumes of polite literature in calf, completing the furniture.

"Yes," Mr. Brooke, "this would be a pretty room

with some new hangings, sofas, and that sort of thing. A little bare now."

"No, uncle," said Dorothea, eagerly. "Pray do not speak of altering anything. There are so many other things in the world that want altering – I like to take things as they are. And you like them as they are, don't you?" she added, looking at Mr. Casaubon. "Perhaps this was your mother's room when you were young."

"It was," he said, with a slow bend of the head.

George Eliot

"I shall make jelly," she said, "and keep some [quinces] on a dish here – they smell so delicious." She sighed, not wanting to add that they reminded her of her childhood home in case Mark should be hurt. In these less gracious surroundings she had tried to recapture the atmosphere of her mother's house with bowls of quinces, the fragrance of well polished furniture, and the special Earl Grey tea, but she often realised how different it really was. The vicarage had been built to match the church and the style of the rooms had not yet, and per-haps never would, become fashionable again.

Barbara Pym

I had expected to see chairs and tables swathed in dust-sheets, and dust-sheets too over the great double bed against the wall. Nothing was covered up. There were brushes and combs on the dress-ing-table, scent, and power. The bed was made up, I saw the gleam of white linen on the pillow-case,

and the tip of a blanket beneath the quilted cover-
let. There were flowers on the dressing-table and
on the table beside the bed, flowers too on the
carved mantelpiece, a satin dressing gown lay on a
chair, and a pair of bedroom slippers beneath. For
one desperate moment I thought that something
had happened to my brain, that I was seeing back
into Time, and looking upon the room as it used to
be, before she died.... In a minute Rebecca herself
would come back into the room, sit down before
the looking-glass at her dressing-table, humming
a tune, reach for her comb and run it through her
hair. If she sat there I should see her reflection in
the glass, and she would see me too....

Daphne de Maurier

The lofty room was painted a pale mauve, a varia-
tion of the elegiac color of Joanna's library, a color
reiterated in the mauve-and-white fabric trellised
with green that draped the bed, a splended lit a la
polonaise that stood slightly aloof from the whole
and yet which was married to the rest through the
pattern of the fabric. From each of its four corners
a luxurious swag traveled upward, only to be re-
united in a circular mauve crown that seemed
magically suspended from the ceiling.... My gaze
traveled to the shadow cast by the bed upon the
fine needlepoint carpet, with its intricate pattern
of fleur-de-lis, then to the bedspread and pillows
embroidered with Joanna's initials.

Francesca Stanfill

After their marriage Joe installed his girl-wife in a vast Park Avenue apartment with white wall-to-wall carpeting, gold furniture, and pictures that were copies of Watteau at his sexiest. Norma's bedroom had an outsized bed with an ermine throw, a mountain of maribou cushions, and a telephone covered by a fancy doll. The apartment boasted every item of an opulent love nest.

Anita Loos

By degrees, I was allowed to see the house. In the sitting room – a large comfortable place with huge sofas and a lot of colour – there were Impressionist paintings, two Renoirs, a Modigliani, a Roualt, and, best of all, a most touching, tender, appealing "still life" by Bonnard of a jug of poppies and meadow sweet. . . . Here were her book shelves, the cupboards with tennis racquets and the old mackintoshes, the pad with the telephone numbers written in her square, capital lettering. So this was where the "Divina" lived.

Cecil Beaton on Greta Garbo's house in Hollywood

It takes a hundred men to make an encampment, but one woman can make a home.

R. G. Ingersoll

The best bedroom in the house, a corner room, sunny, overlooking the main street of Amherst in front. . . . Here in this white-curtained, high-ceilinged room, a red-haired woman with hazel eyes and a contralto voice wrote poems about volcanoes, deserts, eternity, suicide, physical passion, wild beasts, rape, power, madness, separation, the daemon, the grave. Here, with a darning needle, she bound these poems–heavily emended and often in variant versions–into booklets, secured with darning thread, to be found and read after her death. Here she knew "freedom," listening from above-stairs to a visitor's piano-playing, escaping from the pantry where she was mistress of the household bread and puddings, watching, you feel, watching ceaselessly, the life of sober Main Street below.

Adrienne Rich, on the bedroom of Emily Dickinson

The pleasantest room in the house was set aside for Beth, and in it was gathered everything that she most loved, –flowers, pictures, her piano, the little worktable, and the beloved pussies. Father's best books found their way there, mother's easy-chair, Jo's desk, Amy's finest sketches; and every day Meg brought her babies on a loving pilgrimage, to make sunshine for Aunty Beth. John quietly set apart a little sum, that he might enjoy the pleasure of keeping the invalid supplied with the fruit she loved and longed for. . . . and from across the sea came little gifts and cheerful letters, seeming to bring breaths of warmth and fragrance from lands that knew no winter.

Louisa May Alcott

The room was sparsely furnished, the three windows giving onto the Seine were hung with pale blue and white striped unlined taffeta curtains.

Dappled light from the river shone in through the windows past great six-foot-tall branches of white lilacs, which stood before the simple windows.

Billy Baldwin describing Pauline De Rothschild's Paris apartment

Madame de Rambouillet began at the beginning: she designed and built a house in Paris suitable for the form of gathering she was to inaugurate. . . . It was a complete departure from the existing type of nobleman's residence, where the reception-rooms, painted dark brown or red, were so pompous, huge and dreary that it had become the fashion for women to receive in their bedrooms, since these were the only intimate places in the house. Madame de Rambouillet designed a series of small sitting-rooms leading out of each other and giving on to a beautiful garden filled, in summer, with orange and oleander trees; the rooms were cozy; they inspired confidences and long leisurely hours of talk. . . . When Madame de Rambouillet's house was ready, she filled it with people chosen because they could talk amusingly.

Nancy Mitford

Josephine's apartment was remarkable only for its lack of taste and harmony. The furniture is of all colors and all styles; it's a mass of baubles quite devoid of simple elegance or anything artistic—no souvenirs, everything is recent. Fashion is all powerful in Paris and here it reigns supreme. . . .

Gerard Hubert on the Empress Josephine

Every detail of decoration seemed to have been thought out with loving care. Never had wealth of adornment been more daintily disguised in order to be translated into elegance, to be expressive of taste and incite to voluptuousness. Everything there would have warmed the blood of the chilliest mortal. The iridescence of the hangings, whose colour changed as the eye looked at them from different angles, now white, now wholly pink, harmonized with the effects of light infused into the diaphanous folds of the muslin and produced an impression of mistiness. The human soul is strangely attracted to white, love has a delectation for red, and gold gives encouragement to the passions because it has the power to realize their dreams. Thus all that is vague and mysterious in man, all his unexplained affinities, found their involuntary sympathies gratified in this boudoir. There was in this perfect harmony a concerto of colour to which the soul responded with ideas which were at once voluptuous, imprecise and fluctuating.

Honoré de Balzac

One would have imagined that a gentlewoman would have her "things," those objects – photographs, books, souvenirs collected on holiday – which can make a room furnished with other people's furniture into a kind of home. But Jessie seemed to have none of these. . . . The only books to be seen were the library book Jessie happened to be reading at that moment, a paper-backed detective novel that anybody might have and, rather oddly, an old A.B.C. There were no books of devotion, not even a Bible or a prayer-book, which one might certainly have expected a spinster to possess. The "objects" were even more unpromising – an ugly little china dog of some Scottish breed attached to an ash-tray, an old willow-pattern bowl with no apparent purpose, some dusty sea-shells in a box – it seemed almost as if Jessie had been at pains to suppress or conceal her personality. For there was no doubt that she had personality of an uncomfortable kind. . . .

Barbara Pym

"I would not for a throne renounce the occupations of my room."

Geoffrey Scott quoting Mme. de Charrière (Zélide)

A Companionable Solitude

All now was ready; and when it was evening and the innumerable silver sconces were lit and the light airs which for ever moved about the galleries stirred the blue and green arras, so it looked as if the hunstmen were riding and Daphne were flying; when the silver shone and lacquer glowed and wood kindled; when the carved chairs held their arms out and dolphins swam on the walls with mermaids on their backs; when all this and much more than all this was complete and to his liking, Orlando walked through the house with his elk hounds following and felt content.... Yet, as he paraded the galleries he still felt that something was lacking. Chairs and tables, however richly gilt and carved, sofas, resting on lions' paws with swans' necks curving under them, beds even of the softest swansdown are not by themselves enough. People sitting in them, people lying in them improve them amazingly.

Virginia Woolf

Home is not where you live, but where they understand you.

Christian Morgenstern

Whatever brawls disturb the street,
There should be peace at home.

Isaac Watts

The very heart of a home is intimacy. For this is where we are most ourselves. And when we have the inner calm, this is when we give the best parts of ourselves.

Nancy Lindemeyer

The boudoir, was the centre of the house, a carven and gilded wooden paneling replaced the stiff marble of the more formal apartments; there were soft silken hangings instead of stiff satin and heavy brocades. A mat cream, a delicate cherry, a pale blue prevailed. The whole interior was designed to form an appropriate setting for women in the springtime of life, for pleasant and intimate gatherings, for cheerful unconcern.

Nowhere else did the playfulness of spirit which prevailed among the French high nobility just before the troublous days of the Revolution find so unalloyed an expression. For all time the Little Trianon will remain the most refined, the most fragile and yet the most indestructible shrine of this essentially artificial blossoming. The zenith and the nadir of the Rococo, maturing to a climax in the last hour before its death, is, even in our own day, best symbolized by the little clock placed in the centre of the chimney-piece in Marie Antoinette's boudoir.

At the Little Trianon Marie Antoinette felt really at home.

Stefan Zweig writing on Marie Antoinette

My idea of a home is a house in which each member of the family can on the instant kindle a fire in his or her private room.

Ralph Waldo Emerson

> . . . . But every house where love abides,
> And friendship is a guest,
> Is surely home, and home, sweet home;
> For there the heart can rest.

Henry van Dyke

The best testimony to the kind of hospitality which radiated from the household came perhaps from Lady Burne-Jones's nephew, Rudyard Kipling, who often stayed at The Grange when he was a child. After Burne-Jones died, Kipling hung the iron doorbell from The Grange outside his own house in the hope that the happiness which he had felt on ringing it would be passed on to other children. For him The Grange had been a paradise where the world of grown-ups and children mingled amidst paint and pictures, fun and games and music and poetry.

Susan Lasdun

. . . There's no We at an instant,
only Thou and I, two regions
of protestant being which nowhere overlap:
a room is too small, therefore,

if its occupants cannot forget at will
that they are not alone, too big
if it gives them any excuse in a quarrel
for raising their voices.

W. H. Auden

The ornament of a house is the friends who fre-
quent it.

Ralph Waldo Emerson

Blessed be the spot, where cheerful guests retire
To pause from toil, and trim their ev'ning fire;
Blest that abode, where want and pain repair,
And every stranger finds a ready chair.

Oliver Goldsmith

The happiest moments of my life have been the
few which I have passed at home in the bosom of
my family.

Thomas Jefferson

The gaiety of this place is wonderful, think of us
having 25 people on Monday and 18 last night, all
different yet this is thought to be a retired place. . . .
Our family party is so well constituted that we
amuse each other very well.

John Harden

May the gods grant you all things which your heart desires, and may they give you a husband and a home and gracious concord, for there is nothing greater and better than this – when a husband and wife keep a household in oneness of mind, a great woe to their enemies and a joy to their friends, and win high renown.

Homer

There is the domesticity of those who always live alone and can make a precise nest with only those objects they want in it. There is the domesticity of those who finally find a place of their own and gratefully settle into it. There is the domesticity of the family, a noisy, compromising state so in-grained that I barely can remember how much I enjoyed living by myself. . . . When I am drowsing in the dark, in the depths of my old bed in the back of my house, when I know the children are asleep in their beds and the dog is curled up on the floor next to me, I am entirely at home in a setting as fa-miliar and disheveled as an old bathrobe.

Laura Green

Let me step into a house at the close of day
That is littered with children's toys,
And dwell once more in the haunts of play,
With echoes of by-gone noise.

Give me the house where the toys are seen,
The house where children romp,
And I'll happier be than man has been
'Neath the gilded dome of pomp.

Edgar A. Guest

I have a great deal of company in my house; especially in the morning, when nobody calls.

Henry David Thoreau

> The many doth make the household,
> But only one the home.

James Russell Lowell

> The frost performs its secret ministry,
> Unhelped by any wind. The owlet's cry
> Came loud – and hark, again! loud as before.
> The inmates of my cottage, all at rest,
> Have left me to that solitude, which suits
> Abstruser musing: save that at my side
> My cradled infant slumbers peacefully. . . .

Samuel Taylor Coleridge

Not enough has been said about the value of a life lived alone in that it is lived in a house with an open door, with room for the stranger, for the new friend to be taken in and cherished.

May Sarton

It is magnificent when we have company and when alone, it seems to be only a cottage in a beautiful garden. I dine, and breakfast, and sit, all in my own sitting room, and it's most comfortable.

Lady Palmerston of her home at Broadlands

Cissie had given Suzanne the room above the garden. It was a lovely room and in anticipation, Cissie had made it lovelier still. As in all the upper rooms, there was a tiny balcony with an iron rail about – not big enough to sit on but big enough to give an effect of some connection with the outside world. The long windows to this balcony were swung inward and the June scent of the garden filled the room. The room was furnished in maple, that wood which more than any other seems to belong to youth, and Cissie had the walls re-papered with faintest green diagonals against softest tan. An odd green lamp that any girl would love stood on the desk along with a flat bowl of orange pansies and there was a ruffled footstool before the bright chair by the hearth.

"Here's your room," Cissie said, "and nobody's going to bother you in it!"

Neila Gardner White

. . . . every corner in a house, every angle in a room, every inch of secluded space in which we like to hide, or withdraw into ourselves, is a symbol of solitude for the imagination . . . the house shelters daydreaming, the house protects the dreamer, the house allows one to dream in peace.

Gaston Bachelard

I remember dreaming over Bachelard's *The Poetics of Space*. . . . He wrote about the house as a "tool for analysis" of the human soul. By remembering rooms in houses we've lived in, we learn to abide (nice word) within ourselves. I felt close to his sense of the house. He wrote about the strange whir of the sun as it comes into a room in which one is alone.

Frances Mayes

My kitchen linoleum is so black and shiny that I waltz while I wait for the kettle to boil. This pleasure is for the old who live alone. The others must vanish into their expected role.

Florida Scott-Maxwell

Ours yet not ours, being set apart
As a shrine to friendship,
Empty and silent most of the year,
This room awaits from you
What you alone, as visitor, can bring,
A weekend of personal life.
. . .
Felissima notte! May you fall at once
Into a cordial dream, assured
That whoever slept in this bed before
Was also someone we like,
That within the circle of our affection
Also you have no double.

W.H. Auden

My bedroom: *Louis Seize* bed painted white, *toile de Jouy* upholstery on white-painted furniture. Chinese pots containing lilac, plants in earthenware pots and saucers.

Through the shutters the sun pierces and makes incandescent the silver inkpot, the strips of brass inlay on the writing table, and discloses the work of a small spider whose silver thread is weaving a pattern attached to the lilac.

The sound of hundreds of doves on the huge, sloping roof cooing with content....

Cecil Beaton describing his guest room at the home of Pauline and Philippe de Rothschild

The English House

There is nothing quite like the English country-house anywhere else in the world.... the house is essentially part of the country, not only in the country, but part of it, a natural growth.... Irrespective of grandeur and modesty, it should agree with its landscape and suggest the life of its inhabitants past and present and should never overwhelm its surroundings. The peculiar genius of the English country house lies in its knack of fitting in.

Vita Sackville-West

The continued attractiveness of the Georgian interior is no accident of fashion. It typified a period that combined domesticity, elegance, and comfort more successfully than ever before, or, many have argued, since.

Witold Rybczynski

Houses are built to live in and not to look on.

Francis Bacon

The charm, the attraction, character, what you will, of the house is that it has grown over the years in a haphazard sort of way.... It is a conglomeration of style and periods of furniture and decoration.... There is no theme, no connecting style. Each room is a jumble of old and new.

The Duchess of Devonshire on Chatsworth

....the decorator Nicholas Haslam wrote, "Nancy Lancaster decorated these rooms with such panache that they became, and have remained, the model, the very yardstick, of the English style." The English Style, the English Country House Look, the Country House Style, the American Country Style – however it was labeled, its sources were exactly those Nancy had always sought and used. Beginning with a core of Virginian country gentility, she drew from the eighteenth century, from 1920s New York, from Paris and rural France; part haute decor, part simple elegance; a "salad" (as Nancy called it) of fabrics, colors and furniture like the layerings of generations in a house that remained one family's home for centuries, "under-pinnings"; the humble amongst the elevated; a nod toward the "Rules of Taste," yet an accompanying lack of regard for them as well; a balance, a sophisticated architectural preoccupation, warmth, humanity, hospitality, unself-conscious élan.

Robert Becker on Nancy Lancaster

It looks so reasonable, so kindly, so perfectly beautiful, that you feel people might have been making

love and living and dying there, and dear little chil-
dren running about, for the last 1,000 years. . . .
anyway, 600.

Sir Robert Lorrimer

It was an aesthetic education to live within those
walls, to wander from room to room, from the
Soanesque library to the Chinese drawing-room,
adazzle with gilt pagodas and nodding mandarins,
painted paper and Chippendale fret-work, from
the Pompeian parlor to the great tapestry-hung
hall which stood unchanged, as it had been de-
signed two hundred and fifty years before; to sit,
hour after hour, in the pillared shade looking out
on to the terrace.

Evelyn Waugh

Much of the character of every man may be read
in his house.

John Ruskin

Her small Gothic dwelling filled with a strange as-
sortment of objects collected over a long period of
years, crowded with books and pictures and all
kinds of visitors, was, to me . . . a spiritual home.
There was always reading aloud, sketching, visiting
. . . and a lot of laughter.

Cecil Beaton on the home of Edith Olivier

Argyll House, with its soft colours and mellow fur-
niture, was the ideal background against which
Sibyl's guests could look their best, give of their
best, and generally relax in the unassuming and

homely atmosphere. Once through the "great door" set into its gracious early eighteenth-century façade, they entered a broad hall with double doors leading to the garden at the back. The dining room also looked out over the garden. Wood-paneled, it had a country-house atmosphere with its cozy window-seats and capacious fireplace.

Kirsty McLeod on Sibyl Colefax

It turned out to be a greystone manor house, with parrots, lizards, Morris chintzes, and flagstones. The long, paneled drawing room created a comfortable and informal air with its enormous soft chairs, bowls of fat hyacinths, sweet smelling freesias and an untidy litter of books.

Cecil Beaton on Wilsford Manor, the home of Stephen Tennant

Visiting Reddish in the late 1950s was like visiting heaven. I had never seen anything like it; it felt slightly illegal. The drawing room walls were covered in blackberry coloured velvet secured by gold filigree, the library walls were green and gold, and there was leopard skin covering the chairs in the hall. . . .

Vita Sackville-West

Reddish house . . . presented its extremely formal interior on to a village street. . . . The village life seemed to have a delightful Miss Mitford quality. Moreover, the house was a real house. . . . This was the abode of an adult person. . . .

Cecil Beaton

Not a palace, not a castle, not a museum, but a house – Always called "the house." "I'll come across to the house," "See you at the house at 9.30," "They're going round the house," a constant reminder of what the huge building is for: a place for people to live in.

The Duchess of Devonshire on Chatsworth

I was ushered into one of the prettiest, and one of the most curiously-furnished and old-fashioned sitting-rooms that had ever been my lot to see. Mirrors of all shapes, sizes and designs, lined the walls, so that whichever way I gazed I saw myself looking at myself. What space remained was occupied by pictures, chiefly old, and all of a most interesting character. The mantelpiece was a most original compound of Chinese black-lacquered panels, bearing designs of birds, animals, flowers and fruit in gold relief, which had a very good effect, and on either side of the grate a series of old Dutch tiles, mostly displaying Biblical subjects treated in a [the?] serio-comic fashion that exited at that period, were inlaid. . . . I sat down on a cozy little sofa, with landscapes and figures of the Cipriani period painted on the panels; whilst admiring this curious collection of things the door opened behind me, and turning around I found myself face to face with Dante Gabriel Rossetti.

Henry Treffry Dunn

James looked back to Lamb House, "so russet and humble and so British and so pervaded by boiled mutton and turnips; and yet withal so intensely precious and so calculated to rack me with home-sickness."

Henry James

We shape our buildings; thereafter they shape us.

Winston Churchill

A Matter of Scale

Now that I have built a palace I wish I lived in a cottage.

The First Duke of Westminster

Small and economical houses can be made to secure most of the comforts and many of the refinements of large and expensive ones...

Catherine E. Beecher and Harriet Beecher Stowe

It is sixteen yards by ten, nothing above, so you see how grand it must be; but I can be alone there, or with the King and a few others, so I am happy.

Madame de Pompadour, on the Hermitage, her home at Versailles

Another quite different image is that of the farmhouse or cottage. A certain type of middle-class Victorian liked to think of himself as a sturdy yeoman, uncorrupted by aristocratic nonsense, and a rustic element in tables, chairs, and other furniture, and in ingle-nooks and door-latches, was the result.... It helped produce those stiff-backed chairs and settles which are typical of a certain kind of late Victorian middle-class house, and are usually as uncomfortable as they look.

Mark Girouard

With the size and furniture of the house Mrs. Dash-wood was on the whole well satisfied; for though her former style of life rendered many additions to the latter indispensable, yet to add and improve was a delight to her; and she had at this time ready money enough to supply all that was wanted of greater elegance to the apartments. "As for the house itself, to be sure," said she, "it is too small for our family; but we will make ourselves tolerably comfortable for the present, as it is too late in the year for improvements. Perhaps in the spring, if I have plenty of money, as I dare say I shall, we may think about building. These parlours are both too small for such parties of our friends as I hope to see often collected here; and I have some thoughts of throwing the passage into one of them, with perhaps a part of the other, and so leave the re-mainder of that other for an entrance; this, with a new drawing-room, which may be easily added, and a bed-chamber and garret above, will make it a very snug little cottage. I could wish the stairs were handsome. But one must not expect everything; though I suppose it would be no difficult matter to widen them. I shall see how much I am before-hand with the world in the spring, and we will plan our improvements accordingly."

In the meantime, till all these alterations could be made from the savings of an income of five hun-dred a year by a woman who had never saved in her life, they were wise enough to be contented with the house as it was; and each of them was busy in arranging their particular concerns, and endeavouring, by placing around them their books and other possessions, to form themselves a home.

Jane Austen

No architecture is so haughty as that which is simple.

John Ruskin

My home, then—when I at last find a home—is a cottage: a little room with white-washed walls, and a sanded floor; containing four painted chairs and a table, a clock, a cupboard, with two or three plates and dishes, and a set of tea-things in delf. Above, a chamber of the same dimensions as the kitchen, with a deal bedstead, and chest of drawers; small, yet too large to be filled with my scanty wardrobe. . . .

Charlotte Brontë

This place is a mere pied-a-terre until we can suit ourselves better. . . . In the meantime, this place is a fine lesson in condensation, which, to say the truth, we all needed, Mama being as diffuse and elaborate in her tidiness as I am in my litter; Papa unable to tell a short story; and Papa's daughter, as you, my dear friend, know to your cost, equally unable to write a short letter. Yes, we shall be greatly benefited by the compression—though at present the squeeze sits upon us as uneasily as tight stays, and is almost as awkward-looking. One of my great objections to small rooms is their extreme unbecomingness to a person of my enormity. There I sit in our little parlor, like a blackbird in a goldfinch's cage – filling it; the room seems all me; nevertheless we are really getting very comfortable, and falling into our old habits with all imaginable ease.

Mary Russell Mitford in a letter to Mrs. Hofland, April 1820

Home is home, be it never so homely.

Charles Dickens

A big establishment is one thing I will not have . . . Our house would rather be small, or very small would suit me better, homelike in the truest sense of the word.

Gertrude Vanderbilt Whitney, to her diary in the year The Breakers, her Newport mansion, was completed

We said there wasn't no home like a raft, after all. Other places do seem so cramped up and smothering, but a raft don't. You feel mighty free and easy and comfortable on a raft.

Mark Twain

Small rooms or dwellings discipline the mind; large ones weaken it.

Leonardo da Vinci

For some of us a home is a castle set down in a windy moor, inhabited by drafts; for some a gingerbready seaside villa where, when the wind changes, sand sifts through the cracks under the doors; and for others, it is a manor deep in the countryside or in the shadow of the village bell tower. Some family houses are stylish and grand; others not at all. But that has no importance. What truly counts is the house's prevailing spirit.

Alexandra D'Arnoux

A man's dignity may be enhanced by the house he lives in, but not wholly secured by it; the owner should bring honor to the house, not the house to its owner.

Cicero

It was a tiny house, with a little garden behind, and a lawn about as big as a pocket-handkerchief in front. . . . But inside, it was altogether charming, and the happy bride saw no fault from garret to cellar. To be sure, the hall was so narrow, it was fortunate that they had no piano, for one never could have been got in whole; the dining-room was so small that six people were a tight fit; and the kitchen stairs seemed built for the express purpose of precipitating both servants and china pell-mell into the coal-bin. But once get used to these slight blemishes, and nothing could be more complete, for good sense and good taste had presided over the furnishings, and the result was highly satisfactory. There were no marble-topped tables, long mirrors, or lace curtains in the little parlor, but simple furniture, plenty of books, a fine picture or two, a stand of flowers in the bay-window, and scattered all about, the pretty gifts which came from friendly hands, and were the fairer for the loving messages they brought.

Louisa May Alcott

Joy dwells beneath a humble roof;
Heaven is not built of country seats
But queer little suburban streets.

Christopher Morley

My own house is small and compact, yet of such proportions that after I have been living in it for a while I have the illusion that it is a palace.

Cecil Beaton

I had rather be shut up in a very modest cottage, with my books, my family and a few old friends, dining on simple bacon, and letting the world roll on as it liked, than to occupy the most splendid post which any human power can give.

Thomas Jefferson

We dined in a room they called "The Painted Parlor." It was a spacious octagon, later in design than the rest of the house; its walls were adorned with wreathed medallions, and across its dome prim Pompeian figures stood in pastoral groups. They and satin-wood and ormolu furniture, the carpet, the hanging bronze candle-abrum, the mirrors and sconces, were all a single composition, the design of one illustrious hand. "We usually eat here when we're alone," said Sebastian, "it's so cozy."

Evelyn Waugh

I think of a cabin as a state of mind, the desire for a quiet place where you feel at peace with yourself.

Mickey Kelly

My house is diaphanous, but it is not of glass. It is more of the nature of vapor. Its walls contract and expand as I desire. At times, I draw them close about me like protective armor.... But at others, I let the walls of my house blossom out in their own space, which is infinitely extensible.

Georges Spyridaki

"For my own part," said he, "I am excessively fond of a cottage; there is always so much comfort, so much elegance about them. And I protest, if I had any money to spare, I should buy a little land and build one myself, within a short distance of London, where I might drive myself down at any time, and collect a few friends about me, and be happy. I advise every body who is going to build, to build a cottage. My friend Lord Courtland came to me the other day on purpose to ask my advice, and laid before me three different plans of Bonomi's. I was to decide on the best of them. "My dear Courtland," said I, immediately throwing them all into the fire, "do not adopt either of them, but by all means build a cottage."

Jane Austen

A middle-aged bachelor hardly needed thirty rooms to play in, even if one of them boasted a Chien Lung wallpaper. Nast's apartment was designed as a mise-en-scene. Like Jay Gatsby, he had created a palace of hospitality "where he dispensed starlight to casual moths."

Caroline Seebohm writing on Condé Nast

I was born in a cottage, and it seems as though I'm going to end my life in one.

Nancy Lancaster

Indoors and Out

No house should ever be on any hill or anything. It should be of the hill, belonging to it, so hill and house could live together each the happier for the other.... Any house should be beautiful in California in the way California is beautiful.

Frank Lloyd Wright

Like daubs of brilliant Georgian radiance on the huge green landscape, in rough, sometimes hostile but always breathtaking locations, these English-style mansions thinly dotted the Crown territory, popping out from a bluff, nestled in a dip of land or settled regally under a magnificent grove of ancient oak trees. They were called Hundred, Flower de Hundred, Shelly, Shirley, Clover Hill...and they were the physical embodiment of all things Virginian and all attributes Virginians admired: both refined and rugged, inspired yet languid in the tropical heat, formal but comfortable and at ease. They were the concrete expressions of elegant, genteel men of the soil. Through the years the houses became clapboard-and-beam memoirs of their families and their epoch....

Robert Becker on Nancy Lancaster

The little house, as Glennard strolled up to it between the trees, seemed no more than a gay tent pitched against the sunshine. It had the crispness of a freshly starched summer gown, and the geraniums on the verandah bloomed as simultaneously as the flowers in a bonnet. The garden was prospering absurdly. Seed they had sown at random – amid laughing countercharges of incompetence – had shot up in fragrant defiance of all their blunders. He smiled to see the clematis unfolding its punctual wings about the porch. The tiny lawn was as smooth as a shaven cheek, and a crimson rambler mounted to the nursery window of a baby who never cried. A breeze shook the awning above the tea-table, and his wife, as he drew near, could be seen bending above a kettle that was just about to boil. So vividly did the whole scene suggest the painted bliss of a stage setting, that it would hardly have been surprising to see her step forward among the flowers and trill out her virtuous happiness from the verandah rail.

Edith Wharton

I got up at six and watered, then restored myself and the house to our old communion by arranging two glorious bunches of flowers, a celebration of summer. Here on the mantel it is foxglove, honeysuckle, a huge Peace rose, a white Martagon lily, some branches of the small white clematis, and a branch of that bright pink single rose that flowers only once a season.

May Sarton

A house full of books and a garden of flowers.

Andrew Lang

Everywhere the odor of boxwood, like that of Palm Sunday, left one intoxicated.

Jean-Marie Perouse de Montclos on Versailles

It was a very low-key little ad tucked away in the Connecticut column of the real estate section, where hyperbole is the mother tongue, and it struck a wondrously peaceful note. SMALL HOUSE ON THE WATER read the headline above a dim photo of a rather scruffy bit of lawn and an indistinct stretch of water.... We entered a small foyer and squeezed past a monumental piece of furniture into a darkish room dominated by a Franklin stove.... Then beyond the masses of boxes packed and ready for the movers, past the piles of books and magazines and through the glass doors –at the very same moment–Anne and I saw the picture in the ad, liberated from newsprint fuzziness. There was the lawn, not scruffy at all, just a stretch of pale green September grass sloping down to the water, and the water itself, bright blue and studded with white sails. The whole scene was framed by a curve of windswept grasses, overhung with sunshine and gulls and smelling of salt.

Jean Kinkead Martine

I have always spent the autumn in a French country house which I will call the Chateau de Sainte Foy. It occupies one side of a square on the other

side of which are farm buildings; the whole sur-
rounds the basse-cour, where lively, noisy peasants
in blue overalls, horses and big wooden farm carts,
a herd of cows, tractors and the farmer's own little
motor go endlessly to and fro under a tower which
dates from the time of Henri IV. In front of the
house there is a wooden park instersected by
canals, containing two ancient chapels, a dovecote,
a kitchen garden and a charmille, or hornbeam av-
enue, without which no French park is complete.

Nancy Mitford

Green-gold, the garden leaps into the room,
the room leans out into the garden's
hanging intertwine of willows. Voluptuous
on canvas, arum lilies' folded cream
rises on its own green undertone. The walls
are primrose; needlepoint-upholstered
walnut and, underfoot, a Bokhara heirloom
bring in the woodwind resonance of autumn.
Mirrored among the jungle blooms'
    curled crimson
and chartreuse, above the mantel, diva-throated
tuberoses, opening all the stops, deliver
Wagnerian arias of perfume.

Amy Clampitt

I stood looking out the back window of one of the
those old brownstone houses in the East Thirties
which always make an Englishman feel homesick.
It was one of the windows of what is known, for
some curious reason, as a "duplex apartment"–a

misleading phrase which somehow suggests that there is something wrong with it, that it is, for example, inhabited by spies. But whatever the duplicity of the apartment there was nothing duplex about the garden onto which it looked.

Beverley Nichols

I woke to the meadow bright silver with frost, and brilliant sunlight through yellow leaves over the barn. What would I do without this calming open space to rest my eyes on?

May Sarton

Isn't it true that a pleasant house makes winter more poetic, and doesn't winter add to the poetry of the house? The white cottage sat at the end of a little valley, shut in by rather high mountains, and it seemed to be swathed in shrubs.

Gaston Bachelard

Here he lives in soulful reverie . . . his imagination lingering over the still more perfect relationships recently made between new plantings and the ever brilliant Midi sky. He ponders the seasons, the sundial, all manner of new floral species for growing in pots and placement in the pergola. He dreams of secret corridors that could be opened in the overgrown brushwood and the shrubs that need to be trimmed. He takes pleasure in visualizing the closed house lost in slumber while awaiting the return of its master.

Françoise Mohrt writing on Givenchy's Clos Fiorentina

The overall effect of the garden is rather like a Rousseau jungle: but a controlled jungle which is inhabited by little monkeys who swing down to my terrace when I breakfast and perch on the table, begging for handouts, which I give them with pleasure.

Oliver Messel describing the garden at this home Maddox in Barbados

Down here this morning in my white kitchen
along the slim body
of the light,
the narrow body that would otherwise
say forever
the same thing,
the beautiful interruptions, the things
    of this world, twigs
and powerlines, eaves and ranking
branches burn
all over my walls.

Jorie Graham

"It is so little and so high above everything," she said, "that it is almost like a nest in a tree. The slanting ceiling is so funny. See, you can scarcely stand up at this end of the room, and when the morning begins to come I can lie in bed and look right up into the sky through that flat window in the roof. It is like a square patch of light. If the sun is going to shine, little pink clouds float about, and I feel as if I could touch them. And if it rains, the drops patter and patter as if they were saying something nice. Then if there are stars, you can lie and try to count how many go into the patch. It takes such a lot. . . .

You see, it's really a beautiful little room."

Frances Hodgson Burnett

Inside the snug house, blue willow-ware
plates go round the dado, cross-stitch
domesticates the guest room, whole nutmegs
inhabit the spice rack, and when there's fog
or a gale, we get a fire going, listen
to Mozart, read Marianne Moore. . . .

Amy Clampitt

I bought "Merry Hall" for a number of reasons, and one of the most compelling of these reasons was its enchanting name . . . To me, the name meant laughter, and parties on the lawn, and sunlight through the windows; it meant "la vie en rose." And that is how it was.

Beverley Nichols

In Nahant, the ocean waits at the end of every street, alive and huge. Around the town nearly a hundred ships have died. . . . With time, I have come to love the West–the long smile of it, its honesty, its enormous emptiness. But although I live here, I do not live here. I wonder if I ever will. Real homes are built of stories, and the stories I love most are of a little wooden town cupped in the vast hand of the sea.

Brian Doyle

Sibyl happily set to work planning it all. Her photographs reveal, inside the house, an admirably understated approach to the decoration, with faded chintz, rush mats or turkey runners on the floor and tapestries for the bare stone walls. In the drawing-room logs on the hearth and piles of books laid out on old oak tables made what could have been a barrack-like space more homely. In all the rooms there was evidence of Sibyl's joy in collecting as she began to fill Old Buckhurst with the appropriate Tudor furniture. Outside, the open-sided barn became a summer loggia, a sheltered retreat for coolish evenings, its stone flags covered in rush matting, pots of agapanthus scattered among the cane chairs replacing the gloomy ivy, roses and honeysuckle climbed the brick walls to scent the bedroom windows, while madonna lilies stretched their necks in a sunny spot underneath. Along the length of the house a wide paved terrace was laid, with a plant-smothered wall and shallow steps down to an expanse of lawn, perfect for perambulating guests.

Kirsty McLeod on Sibyl Colefax

She rose from the writing-table where, list in hand, she had been going over the wedding-invitations, and walked toward the drawing-room window. Everything about her seemed to contribute to that rare harmony of feeling which levied a tax on every sense. The large coolness of the room, its fine traditional air of spacious living, its outlook over field and woodland toward the lake lying under the silver bloom of September, the very scent of the late violets in a glass on the writing-table; the rose-mauve masses of hydrangeas in tubs along the terrace; the fall, now and then, of a leaf through the still air – all, somehow, were mingled in the suffusion of well-being that yet made them seem so much dross upon its current.

Edith Wharton

I really lived in that drawing room. I would sit there in the summertime with the doors and windows open. It was simply lovely. And you could walk right through to the garden. All of Haseley was that way. You could open it up end to end and let the summer air go right through.

Robert Becker on Nancy Lancaster

The five tiglio trees, old world lindens or limes, bear no fruit. They provide shade along the broad terrace beside the house when the sun will not allow us on the front terrace. We have lunch under the tigli almost every day. Their blossoms are like pearly earrings dangling from the leaves, and when they open – all it seems on the same day – fragrance envelops the whole hillside. At the height of the bloom, we sit on the upstairs patio, just adjacent to the trees, trying to identify the fragrance. I think it smells like the perfume counter in the dime store; Ed thinks it smells like the oil his uncle Syl used to slick back his hair. Either way, it attracts every bee in town.

Frances Mayes

Housekeeping

Lucy came running full tilt downstairs, having just nipped into the drawing-room to smooth a cover, to straighten a chair, to pause a moment and feel whoever came in must think how clean, how bright, how beautifully cared for, when they saw the beautiful silver, the brass fire-irons, the new chair-covers, and the curtains of yellow chintz; she appraised each; heard a roar of voices; people already coming up from dinner; she must fly!

Virginia Woolf

Thursday came: all work had been completed the previous evening; carpets were laid down, bed-hangings festooned, radiant white counterpanes spread, toilet tables arranged, furniture rubbed, flowers piled in vases: both chambers and saloons looked as fresh and bright as hands could make them. The hall, too, was scoured; and the great carved clock, as well as the steps and banisters of the staircase, were polished to the brightness of glass: in the dining room, the side-board flashed resplendent with plate; in the drawing-room and boudoir, vases of exotics bloomed on all sides.

Charlotte Brontë

A house that shines from the care it receives appears to have been rebuilt from the inside; it is as though it were new inside.... Through housewifely care a house recovers not so much its originality as its origin. And what a great life it would be if, every morning, every object in the house could be made anew by our hands.

Gaston Bachelard

Mildred is here cleaning. I think of all the years since she first began to come here and how her presence, so quiet, humorous, and distinguished, has blessed all that is here. The solitude is animated but not broken. I sit at my desk and work better because I know her sensitive hands are busy dusting and making order again.

May Sarton

Housekeeping ain't no joke.

Louisa May Alcott

Perhaps it is not too frivolous to say that the best clue to the scale of life at Windsor was the number of dusters which were needed: twelve hundred were ordered each year and that was only a quarter of the number which were in constant circulation.

Susan Lasdun

When I find a man who keeps his cigars in the coal-scuttle, his tobacco in the toe end of a Persian slipper, and his unanswered correspondence transfixed by a jack-knife into the very centre of his wooden mantelpiece, then I begin to give myself virtuous airs.... Our chambers were always full of chemicals and criminal relics which had a way of wandering into unlikely positions, and of turning up in the butter-dish or in even less desirable places.

Arthur Conan Doyle, writing of the rooms of Sherlock Holmes

Picture to yourself the darkest, most disorderly place imaginable...blotches of moisture condensed on the ceiling; an oldish grand piano, on which the dust disputed the place with various pieces of engraved and manuscript music; under the piano (I do not exaggerate) an unemptied chamber pot; beside it a small walnut table accustomed to the frequent overturning of the secretary placed upon it; a quantity of pens encrusted with ink....then more music. The chairs, mostly cane-seated, were covered with plates bearing the remains of last night's supper.

Baron de Tremont, describing the workroom of Beethoven

There was a fire burning in the pinched little grate. Walls distempered, the distemper flaking badly in patches....Indifferent watercolors of the Roman Campagna, trout pools, etc., in cheap gilt frames. One rather good veneered Queen Anne bureau and one fake lacquer bureau. In the window a statuette of himself by Paul Troubetskoy. On the mantelpiece a late Staffordshire figure of Shakespeare, a china house, the lid of which forms a box. Only a few conventionally-bound classics plus Osbert Sitwell's latest publication prominently displayed on a table. Two stiff armchairs before the fire and brass fender. A shoddy three-ply screen attached to the fireplace to shelter from draughts anyone sitting between the fire and the doorway.

James Lee-Milne on Shaw's Corner, the home of George Bernard Shaw

Although the Misses Bede had a maid they were both quite domesticated and helped her in various small ways, clearing away the breakfast things, dusting their own bedrooms and doing a little cooking when they felt like it. On this particular morning, however, which was the day of the vicarage garden party, Belinda decided that she could miss doing her room with a clear conscience, as there were so many more important things to be done. It was unlikely that Miss Liversidge would be visiting them and putting them to shame by writing "E. Liversidge" with her finger, as she had once done when Emily had neglected to dust the piano. Typical of Edith, of course, going straight to the point with no beating about the bush. Not that she could talk either, with dog's hairs all over the carpet and the washing-up left overnight.

Barbara Pym

Home, you say, when day is done,
Home to comfort and peace and rest;
Home, where the children romp and run –
There is the place that you love the best!
Yet what would the home be like if you
Had all of its endless tasks to do?

Would it be home if she were not there,
Brave and gentle and fond and true?
Could you so fragrant a meal prepare?

Could you the numberless duties do?
What were the home that you love so much,
Lacking her presence and gracious touch?

She is the spirit of all that's fair;
She is the home that you think you build;
She is the beauty that you dream of there;
She is the laughter with which it's filled –
She, with her love and her gentle smile,
Is all that maketh the home worth while.

Edgar A. Guest

Kids pursue comfort at the expense of your house. Concepts like order and responsibility fly over their heads like geese flying north in the spring. Beauty is something they pursue with mascara and purple eyeshadow.

We end up in twenty-year wars with our children over the way our houses look. Children simply don't care. What they ask of life is something interesting to do for a while and then a place to sprawl.

The thing is, I can understand being a kid. I remember when the whole world, especially my parents' ordinary living room, seemed inviting. I played hide-and-seek behind chairs. I'd invent dramas for the china figurines. My brother and I built long winding roads out of books, on which we drove his model cars.

.... So how do we live with the chaos, the ordinary mess generated by the children who live with us? The answer has to be: by remembering, by forgiving, and by drawing the line.

Mary Beth Danielson

"Hominess" is not neatness.

Witold Rybczynski

I don't blame children for fleeing those . . . houses, nonshelters, dehumanized, ostentatious, rarely expressing an individual family's way of life. When I was writing a column for *Family Circle* I had planned one in praise of shabbiness. A house that does not have one worn, comfy chair in it is soulless. It all comes back to the fact that we are not asked to be perfect, only human. What a relief it is to walk into a human house!

May Sarton

Prudence prided herself on being a good hostess and tried to think of everything that a guest could possibly need. Jane, while appreciating this and benefiting from it, thought the flat a little too good to be true. Those light satin striped covers would "show the dirt"—the pretty Regency couch was really rather uncomfortable and the whole place was so tidy that Jane felt out of place in it. Her old schoolboy's camel-hair dressing-gown looked as unsuitable in Prudence's spare-room as Prudence's turquoise blue wool housecoat did at the vicarage.

Barbara Pym

. . . . Spotless rooms
where nothing's left lying about

chill me, so do cups used for ashtrays or smeared
with lipstick: the homes I warm to,

though seldom wealthy, always convey a feeling
  of bills being promptly settled

with checks that don't bounce.

W. H. Auden

I had previously taken a journey to S—, to purchase some new furniture: my cousins having given me carte blanche to effect what alterations I pleased, and a sum having been set aside for that purpose.... Dark handsome new carpets and curtains, an arrangement of some carefully selected antique ornaments in porcelain and bronze, new coverings, and mirrors, and dressing-cases for the toilet tables, answered the end: they looked fresh without being glaring. A spare parlour and bedroom I refurnished entirely, with old mahogany and crimson upholstery: I laid canvas on the passage, and carpets on the stairs. When all was finished, I thought Moor House as complete a model of bright modest snugness within, as it was, at this season, a specimen of wintry waste and dreariness without.

Charlotte Brontë

Everyone still awoke to a fire—the Kelmarsh housemaids slipped in and lit them at dawn—but radiators took the nip out of the air as well, and kept the rooms dry, while fitted carpets and rugs covered cold, bare floors.... At the foot of the generous four-poster beds there would be a chaise longue or a deep-seated chair with an ottoman to stretch out on before dinner. More chairs surrounded the fire.

Each room had a desk with ample Kelmarsh Hall writing paper; each had books and a reading lamp at every possible resting spot. There was always a bottle of drinking water and a glass next to the bed, and every room always displayed an abundance of fresh flowers from the garden.

Robert Becker on Nancy Lancaster

And so there began a soundless passing to and fro through swing doors of aproned white-capped maids, handmaidens not of necessity, but adepts in a mystery of grand deception practised by host-esses in Mayfair from one-thirty to two, when, with a wave of the hand, the traffic ceases, and there rises instead this profound illusion in the first place about food – how it is not paid for; and then that the table spreads itself voluntarily with glass and silver, little mats, saucers of red fruit; films of brown cream mask turbot; in casseroles severed chickens swim; coloured, undomestic, the fire burns; and with the wine and the coffee (not paid for) rise jocund visions before musing eyes; gently speculative eyes; eyes to whom life appears musical, mysterious; eyes now kindled to observe genially the beauty of the red carnations which Lady Bruton (whose movements were al-ways angular) had laid beside her plate. . . .

Virginia Woolf

Coming Home

Where we love is home,
Home that our feet may leave, but not our hearts.

Oliver Wendell Holmes

The great advantage of a hotel is that it's a refuge
from home life.

George Bernard Shaw

Housed everywhere but nowhere shut in, that is
the motto of the dreamer of dwellings.

Gaston Bachelard

What's the good of a home if you are never in it?

George Grossmith

It was sad coming back alone to an empty house. . . .
Ianthe had always wanted a house of her own and
as soon as she had shut the door behind her she
forgot the lonely homecoming in the pleasure she
still felt at seeing her furniture and possessions in
their new setting. Here were the Hepplewhite chairs
and the Pembroke table, coveted by Mervyn
Cantrell, portraits of her grandparents and of her

father in cope and biretta, the corner cupboard with the lustre jugs collected by her mother, the old silky Bokhara rugs on the polished parquet floor of the sitting room, the familiar books in the white-painted bookshelves, and the china ornaments she remembered from childhood.

Barbara Pym

A man travels the world over in search of what he needs and returns home to find it.

George Moore

The rooms we talk and work in
     always look injured
When trunks are being packed, and when,
     without warning,
We drive up in the dark, unlock and switch
     lights on,
They seem put out. . . .

W. H. Auden

I lived in the city, but it was my family's old house in Caldwell I still called "home." The bus dropped me off on the main street and, if the weather was clear, I walked the two blocks up the hill to the house, a walk familiar to me for decades. There had been some changes since I was a child. But the houses themselves, the big old trees, and most of the people I met were the same. After the liveliness of the city Caldwell seemed hushed and still, as though it had been fixed in the amber of time. Maybe that's why I remember those walks as if every one of them were lit with the sharply slanted golden sun of the late summer's long evening; as if it were always that moment when daylight is lingering long beyond its time, poignant and miraculous.

Suzanne Fox

Goethe once said, "He is happiest, king or peasant, who finds his happiness at home." And Goethe knew—because he never found it.

Elbert Hubbard

Folks had it down that I was a wanderin' man, but most wanderin' men I've known only wandered because of the home they expected to find... hoped to find, I mean.

Louis L'Amour

I am home, I am home, I am home. I have been home for a week so that it is now natural, but my joy is more than natural.

Florida Scott-Maxwell

How sad and empty the house felt when I walked in yesterday afternoon!...A few days of neglect and the soul goes out of the house, that's for sure.

May Sarton

Oh, this coming back to an empty house, Rupert thought, when he had seen her safely up to her door. People—though perhaps it was only women —seemed to make so much of it. As if life itself were not as empty as the house one was coming back to.

Barbara Pym

Wherever smoke, wreaths Heavenward curl –
Cave of a hermit, Hovel of churl,
Mansion of merchant, princely dome –
Out of the dreariness
Into its cheeriness,
Come we in weariness,
Home.

Stephen Chalmers

To me, home always meant Renishaw; and the summer took me there. . . . I remember, every year, directly I arrived, running through the cool, pillared hall to the low, painted door a little taller than myself, opposite, and standing on tiptoe, so that the smell of the garden should come at me over it through the open window; the overwhelming and, as it seemed, living scent of stocks and clove carnations and tobacco-plant on a foundation of sun-warmed box hedges, the odor of any component of which to this day carries me back to infancy, though never now do I obtain the full force it drew from that precise combination . . .

Osbert Sitwell

No place is more delightful than one's own fireside.

Cicero

Ah! There is nothing like staying home for real comfort.

Jane Austen

Home was quite a place when people stayed there.

E. B. White

My room is so delicious after a whole day outside, it seems to me that I am not myself except in my room.

Gwen John

I was flying homeward now. Home, home to Caddagat, home to ferny gullies, to the sweet sad rush of many mountain waters, to the majesty of rugged Borgongs; home to dear old granny, and uncle and aunt, to books, to music; refinement, company, pleasure, and the dear old homestead I love so well.

Sybylla Melvyn

As much as I converse with sages and heroes that have very little of my love and admiration, I long for rural and domestic scenes, for the warbling of birds and prattling of my children.

John Adams

Cleave to thine acre: the round year
Will fetch all fruits and virtues here.
Fool and foe may harmless roam,
Loved and lovers bide at home.

Ralph Waldo Emerson

The happiness of the domestic fireside is the first boon of mankind; and it is well it is so, since it is that which is the lot of the mass of mankind.

Thomas Jefferson

The dear place looks so nice & all the rooms up-stairs, are just the same, which made me think of happy days spent here in my childhood...[we] dined in the old Dining Room & sat afterwards in the yellow Drawing room. It seemed to me like a happy dream to be here with my husband.

Queen Victoria, on returning to her home at Claremont
for the first time after her marriage

As a child, I had lived in six houses, in three countries, on two continents. Since then I had occupied seven different homes. I had dreamt of a boat, and escape; but had I not always been running away, or at least moving away? Each shovel of gravel, each nail hammered, each board sawn, settled me more firmly...My house had begun with the dream of a boat. The dream had run aground—I was now rooted in place.

Witold Rybczynski

The only pleasure of coming back to one's own house is the pleasure of unpacking the bibelots one has got elsewhere.

John Singer Sargent

'Mid pleasures and palaces though we may roam, Be it ever so humble, there's no place like home.

John Howard Payne

When I was at home, I was in a better place.

William Shakespeare

Stay at home, and you don't wear out your shoes.

Yiddish Proverb

It was a wild, tempestuous night, towards the close of November. Holmes and I sat together in silence all the evening, he engaged with a powerful lens deciphering the remains of the original inscription on a palimpsest, I deep in a recent treatise on surgery. Outside the wind howled down Baker Street, while the rain beat fiercely against the windows. . . . "Well, Watson, it's as well we have not to turn out tonight," said Holmes, laying aside his lens.

Arthur Conan Doyle

Any old place I hang my hat is home, sweet home to me.

William Jerome and Jean Schwartz

Stay, stay at home, my heart and rest;
Home-keeping hearts are the happiest,
For those that wander they know not where
Are full of trouble and full of care;
To stay at home is best.

Henry Wadsworth Longfellow

Sources

W.H. Auden, Excerpts from *W.H. Auden: Collected Poems*, edited by Edward Mendelson. Copyright 1940 and renewed © 1968 by W.H. Auden. Reprinted with the permission of Random House, Inc.

Jane Austen, *Mansfield Park, Northanger Abbey, Sense and Sensibility*, Magna Classics, 1992

Gaston Bachelard, *The Poetics of Space*, translated from the French by Maria Jolas, New York, Orion Press, 1964

Billy Baldwin, *An Autobiography with Michael Gardine*, Little, Brown and Company, 1985

Cecil Beaton, from Richard Buckle, ed., *Self Portrait with Friends: The Selected Diaries of Cecil Beaton, 1926–1974*, Weidenfeld and Nicholson, London, 1979

Louise Bogan, *Journey Around My Room, The Autobiography of Louise Bogan*, Viking, 1980

Charlotte Brontë, *Jane Eyre*, Penguin Books

Stephen Calloway, *Style Traditions: Recreating Period Interiors* by Stephen Calloway and Stephen Jones, Rizzoli, New York, 1990

Truman Capote, *Other Voices, Other Rooms*, Random House, New York, 1948

Agatha Christie, *Sleeping Murder*, Dodd, Mead & Co., New York, 1976

Amy Clampitt: Excerpts from "Townhouse interior with Cat" and "The Sacred Hearth Fire" from *What the Light Was Like*. Copyright © 1985 by Amy Clampitt. Excerpts from "The Cove," "Meridian," and "On the Disadvantages of Central Heating" from *The Kingfisher*. Copyright © 1979, 1980, 1981, 1982, 1983 by Amy Clampitt. All reprinted with the permission of Alfred A. Knopf, Inc.

Eliza Cook, *The Old Arm-Chair*, D. Lothrop & Co., Boston, 1886

Mary Beth Danielson, "The Mess" and Laura Green, "Bed," from Laurie Abraham, et al., *Reinventing Home: Six Working Women Look At Their Home Lives*, Penguin Books, New York, 1991

Elsie de Wolfe, *The House in Good Taste*, The Century Co., New York, 1913

Duchess of Devonshire, *The House, A Portrait of Chatsworth*, Macmillan Ltd., London

Arthur Conan Doyle, *The Complete Sherlock Holmes*, Doubleday, New York, 1927

Brian Doyle, "Pointing East," Jean Kinkead Martine, "The Love Nest," from *Thoughts of Home: Reflections on Families, Houses, and Homelands from the Pages of House Beautiful*, Hearst Books, New York, 1995

Daphne du Maurier, *Rebecca*, Doubleday Doran and Company, New York, 1938

Henry Treffry Dunn, quoted in Charlotte Gere, *Nineteenth-Century Decoration: The Art of the Interior*, Harry N. Abrams, New York, 1989

George Eliot, *Middlemarch*, The Modern Library, New York, 1992

Suzanne Fox, *Home Life: A Journey Through Rooms and Recollections*, Simon & Schuster, New York, 1997

B.H. Friedman, *Gertrude Vanderbilt Whitney*, Doubleday, Garden City, New York, 1978

Lillian Gish, from *Architectural Digest* (April 1979)

Jorie Graham, "Still Life with Window and Fish" from *Erosion*. Copyright © 1983 by Princeton University Press. Reprinted with the permission of the publisher.

Edgar A. Guest, *The Passing Throng*, The Reilly and Lee Company, Chicago, 1923

Dee Hardie, "Secrets of the Sleeping Porch," *House Beautiful* (August 1992)

Kathryn Chapman Harwood, *The Lives of Vizcaya: Annals of a Great House*, Banyan Books, Miami, 1985

Gervase Jackson-Stops, ed., *Writers at Home*, The National Trust, Trefoil Books, Ltd., London, 1985

Mickey Kelly, "A Charming Case of Cabin Fever" from *Victoria Magazine* (July 1992)

Louis L'Amour, *Treasure Mountain*, Bantam Books, New York, 1984

Nancy Lancaster, quoted in Robert Becker, *Nancy Lancaster: Her Life, Her Work, Her Art*, Alfred A. Knopf, New York, 1996

Clarence John Laughlin, *Ghosts Along the Mississippi: An Essay in the Poetic Interpretation of Louisiana's Plantation Architecture*, Bonanza Books, New York, 1961

Susan Lasdun, (also excerpts by John Harden, Mark Girouard, Queen Victoria, Lady Palmerston and Lady Mount-Temple) from *Victorians at Home*. Copyright © 1981 by Susan Lasdun. Introduction copyright © 1981 by Mark Girouard. Reprinted with the permission of Viking Penguin, a division of Putnam Penguin Inc.

Nancy Lindemeyer, ed., *Victoria, Intimate Home*, Smallwood and Stewart, New York, 1992

Anita Loos, *A Girl Like I*, The Viking Press, New York, 1966

Mary S. Lovell, *Rebel Heart: The Scandalous Life of Jane Digby el Mezrah*, W. W. Norton & Company, New York, 1995

Frances Mayes, *Under the Tuscan Sun*, Broadway Books, New York, 1997

Kirsty McLeod with Sibyl Colefax, *A Passion For Friendship*, Michael Joseph, Ltd, London, 1991

Suzy Menkes, *The Windsor Style*, Grafton Books / Collins Publishing Group, London, 1987

Oliver Messel, quoted in Charles Castle, *Oliver Messel: A Biography*, Thames and Hudson, New York and London, 1986

Mary Russell Mitford, *Recollections of a Literary Life*, AMS Press, 1975

Nancy Mitford, quoted in Harold Mario Mitchell Acton, *Nancy Mitford: A Memoir*, Harper & Row, New York, 1975. Also *The Water Beetle*, Atheneum Publishers, New York, 1962

Françoise Mohrt, *Givenchy Style*, Vendome Press, New York, 1998

George Moore, *The Brook Kerith: A Syrian Story*, Macmillan, New York, 1936

Jan Morris, *Pleasures of a Tangled Life*, Vintage, 1990

Charlottte Moss, *A Passion for Detail*, Doubleday, New York, 1991

Vladimir Nabokov, *Speak, Memory: A Memoir*, Grosset & Dunlap, New York, 1951

Beverley Nichols, *The Gift of a Home*, Dodd, Mead and Co., New York, 1972

Nigel Nicolson, *Portrait of a Marriage*, Atheneum, New York, 1973

Kathleen Norris, *Dakota: A Spiritual Geography*, Houghton Mifflin Company, New York, 1993

Patrick O'Higgins, *Madame: An Intimate Biography of Helena Rubinstein*, The Viking Press, New York, 1971

Edgar Allan Poe, "The Fall of the House of Usher" and "The Masque of the Red Death," from *Tales of Mystery and Imagination*, Wordsworth Classics, Ware [England], 1995

Jean-Marie Perouse de Monclos, *Versailles*, Abbeville Press, New York, 1991

Barbara Pym, *Jane and Prudence, An Unsuitable Attachment*, and *Some Tame Gazelle*, Harper & Row, New York, 1981, 1982, and 1986

Agnes Repplier, *Times and Tendencies*, Houghton Mifflin Company, Boston, 1931

Adrienne Rich: "Vesuvius at Home: The Power of Emily Dickinson" from *On Lies, Secrets, and Silence, Selected Prose 1966–1978*, W. W. Norton & Company, New York, 1979.

Witold Rybczynski, *Home: A Short History of an Idea*, and *The Most Beautiful House in the World*, Penguin Books, New York, 1986 and 1990

V. Sackville-West, *English Country Houses*, William Collins Sons, London, 1947

May Sarton, excerpts from *Journal of a Solitude*. Copyright © 1973 by May Sarton. Reprinted with the permission of W. W. Norton & Company, Inc.

Geoffrey Scott, *The Portrait of Zilide*, Charles Scribner's Sons, New York, 1927

Florida Scott-Maxwell, *The Measure of My Days*, Penguin Books, New York, 1979

Caroline Seebohm, *The Man Who Was Vogue: The Life and Times of Condé Nast*, Viking Press, New York, 1982

Jody Shields, "Remembered Rooms" from *The New York Times* (June 7, 1992)

Osbert Sitwell, *Left Hand! Right Hand!*, Macmillan, London, 1944

Jane S. Smith, *Elsie de Wolfe: A Life in High Style*, Atheneum, New York, 1982

Walter Shaw Sparrow, *Our Homes and How to Make the Best of Them*, Hodder & Stoughton, London, 1909

Francesca Stanfill, *Wakefield Hall*, Villard, New York, 1993

William Makepeace Thackeray, *Vanity Fair: Authoritative Text, Backgrounds and Contents, Criticism*, W. W. Norton & Company, New York, 1994

Mark Twain (Samuel Langhorne Clemens), *Huckleberry Finn*, New York: Harper & Brothers, 1896 and *Mark Twain's Letters*, Harper & Brothers, New York, 1917

Katharine Tweed, ed., *The Finest Rooms*, The Viking Press, New York, 1964

Edith Wharton, "Souls Belated" from *Roman Fever and Other Stories*, Charles Scribner's Sons, New York, 1997

Nelia Gardner White, "Smart Girl" from *Harper's Bazaar* (November, 1935)

Palmer White, *Elsa Schiaparelli: Empress of Paris Fashion*, Rizzoli, New York, 1986

Virginia Woolf, *Mrs Dalloway*, *To the Lighthouse*, and *The Waves*, Harcourt Brace & World, New York, 1925, 1927, and 1931

Frank Lloyd Wright, *An Autobiography*, Duell, Sloan and Pearce, New York, 1943

Stefan Zweig, *Marie Antoinette: The Road to the Guillotine*, Garden City Publishing Co., Garden City, New York, 1932

We apologize for any omissions in regards to copyright acknowledgment and upon notification will make the appropriate acknowledgment in subsequent editions.

ACKNOWLEDGMENT:

Special thanks to Benjamin Kaplan and Fred Courtright for their participation in this book.

*M*y brother Major Edward J. Moss, Jr., USMC died at the age of 40 of acute lymphoid leukemia. In his name a part of the proceeds from The Poetry of Home will be donated to The Irvington Institute for Immunological Research.

The Irvington Institute has been a leading pioneer in funding groundbreaking medical research for diseases that touch all of us – lupus, cancer, diabetes, AIDS, rheumatoid arthritis and other immune system disorders. The Irvington Institute funds the most brilliant, promising postdoctoral scientists through its prestigious fellowship program. For every discovery that advances our health and well-being, immunological researchers have laid the foundation for the cure, prevention, and treatment of a disease.

For more information on The Irvington Institute or to make a donation please write to 120 East 56th St., Suite 340, New York, New York 10022, (212) 758-8250.

Charlotte Moss

This book
has been printed from
Diotima & Ariadne types
on Mohawk Superfine paper
by The Stinehour Press.
Designed by
Jerry Kelly.

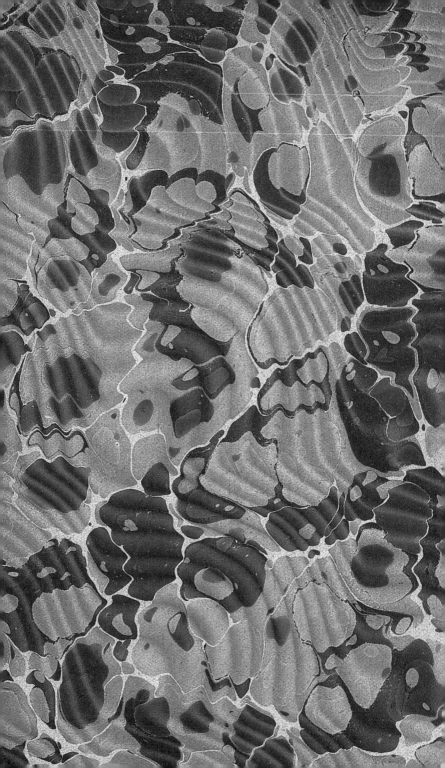